WINTER DEVOTIONS

The Daily Devotion Series

ALAN AND MARY SCHRADER

WINTER DEVOTIONS
The Daily Devotion Series
Published by
IFCA Gospel Express
25595 Chardon Road
Cleveland, OH 44143
www.ifcaBibleCollege.org

EDITED BY ABBIE MOUREY

✾ Created with Vellum

DEDICATION

WE WOULD LIKE TO DEDICATE THIS BOOK TO OUR FIRST DAUGHTER, ANNA JANE.

You are our first daughter, and you are no wimp. You are mighty! You are one who faces life head-on with an incredible can-do attitude. You have remarkable strength and ability to gather resources you need to endure hard and harsh situations. Like the grand tree that faces extreme conditions in the winter months, Anna, you have the ability to flourish in the most challenging situations. We are so thankful for the amazing strength, resilience, and fortitude God has given you. We love you, Anna Jane.

CONTENTS

ABOUT THE AUTHORS

Alan and Mary Schrader live in the Cleveland, Ohio area. Married for over twenty-eight years, they have four children and one grandchild. They've been serving together as pastors for as long as they have been married. Both have served in various full-time ministries since 1987. Alan and Mary have a passion to see people brought into maturity and fruitfulness for the glory of God.

 facebook.com/alan.j.schrader

 instagram.com/pastorajs

 twitter.com/AlanJamesSchra1

 youtube.com/AlanJamesSchrader

FOREWORD

I'm personally persuaded you don't need to limit yourself to just one shower in your lifetime. In fact, I think you can shower more often than only once a year or even once a month.

I'm convinced it's okay to shower in direct proportion to the frequency with which we get dirty. For me, it happens every day. I can't navigate a day without getting sticky or grimy in some manner. Now, what I'm about to say may strike you as a little OCD, but the truth is I shower daily. I know, I know, that seems a bit obsessive. But in my case, I've had to accept the fact that I need to shower every day.

I feel the same way about *spiritual* cleansing. I find that, simply by doing life, I get defiled spiritually every day. I like to get cleansed spiritually in direct proportion to the frequency with which I get defiled. Therefore, I enjoy getting cleansed spiritually *every* day.

Furthermore, I'm personally persuaded you don't need to

limit yourself to just one meal a week. Now, I have no problem with anyone who disagrees with me on this one. But for me, I'm convinced it's okay to eat more than once a week.

In fact, I'm going to take it even further. I think it's okay to eat more than once a day. In my opinion, it's okay to eat as frequently as you get hungry.

I feel the same way about *spiritual* feeding. I believe in feeding ourselves with the Word of God in direct proportion to our spiritual hunger.

Some Christians live on a starvation diet spiritually. They lack a systematic way to feed themselves in the Word during the week, and hope that the diet they get from a pulpit on Sundays will carry them.

Listen, Jesus didn't die for us to live off one meal a week. He died to give us an abundant life in His Word and Spirit. One way to pursue that abundant life is through reading *The Daily Devotion Series*.

The purpose of this series is to sit at Jesus' feet every day, hear His Word, talk to Him, be cleansed in the Spirit, and be strengthened for the war zone of life. God's Word washes us (Ephesians 5:26) and feeds us (Matthew 4:4).

Feeling filthy? Devote yourself to daily cleansing through His Word.

Feeling depleted? Devote yourself every day to eating the words of His mouth.

Don't just read the foreword and introduction to this book. *Do this thing*. Take time every day, with every chapter, to devote yourself to strengthening your relationship with your Best Friend. My dear friends, Alan and Mary Schrader, will guide your journey with skill and understanding.

Happy showering!

Happy feeding!

—Bob Sorge, author, bobsorge.com

INTRODUCTION

Reading *Winter Devotions* will produce a healthy and balanced diet of hope for the discouraged. It will provide a refuge for the hurting and friendship for the lonely.

The four seasons—winter, spring, summer, and fall—offer some great insights for those who take the time to look and observe their beauty. The Creator of the heavens and the earth is neither quiet nor thoughtless as He changes our times and transforms our seasons. How sad to go through the changing seasons of life blindly and drudgingly without discovering the purpose of change!

We all need to be reminded that seasons are God's idea: "He appointed the moon for seasons; the sun knows its going down" (Psalm 104:19). Simply put, seasons are designed to deepen us, to instruct us in the wisdom and ways of our Creator.

The beginning of this series starts with the winter season. In the months of December through February, we pray you would experience nourishment, motivation, and encouragement so that you can flourish in your relationship with the Creator.

For many, winter can be a season of changing moods. Bringing with it frigid temperatures, it can be a time of discomfort, discontentment, and barrenness. Winter can remind us of short days, long nights, and fading memories of fun in the warm sun.

For others, however, winter can be an occasion to slow down and enjoy times in the freshly fallen white snow. If you like to ski, snowboard, snowmobile, or sled, you can't wait for the first heavy snowfall. Some even look forward to winter so they can take that long awaited vacation.

Spiritually speaking, the winter season of life can be difficult to navigate and often discouraging. We can grow cold in our faith and begin to isolate ourselves from our heavenly Father. Winter can also appear to be a fruitless season as nature around us has gone into dormancy.

God wants us to endure through the winter season of life so that we can appreciate His unfailing love in deeper measure. The winter season can be a time of great growth as you walk with God and allow Him to escort you through the cold storms of life. It's been said, "Deeper roots make for stronger lives." So let's make the most of every opportunity and strengthen ourselves with daily devotions.

As you read each devotion, we encourage you to journal. Journaling can be an effective way to help you reach a wide range of goals. Putting your thoughts down on paper not only clears your mind, but it can assist you in making important connections among your thoughts, feelings, and behaviors. It may even buffer and reduce stress. Most importantly, journaling can be a way of talking to God. We want to embolden you to find a daily and consistent retreat so that you can experience the power of meditative prayer and writing in your life.

May you find your Savior opening His arms of love to you as you move through this season. Take your time. Walk slowly. Feel God's presence as you consider the days, weeks, and years that He has given to you. Ask Him to bring new strength to your soul daily.

—Alan and Mary

DECEMBER 1

Hard-Pressed On Every Side?

But we have this treasure in earthen vessels, that the excellence of the power may be of God and not of us. We are hard-pressed on every side, yet not crushed; we are perplexed, but not in despair; persecuted, but not forsaken; struck down, but not destroyed.

— 2 CORINTHIANS 4:7-9

Are you hard-pressed on every side? The apostle Paul used the term *hard-pressed* to convey the idea of being hunted. Paul was a hunted man because of what he was proclaiming about Jesus. In Acts 23:12, forty men conspired together not to eat or drink until they had murdered Paul. Paul knew what it was liked to be hard-pressed.

Looking at our opening scripture, we see Paul not only faced being hard-pressed, but also being perplexed, persecuted, and struck down. The Scriptures are very clear on how we are to overcome these challenges. It has everything to do with having an eternal perspective and knowing God's everlasting plan. That is the only way we can say with Paul,

> Therefore we do not lose heart. Even though our outward man is perishing, yet the inward man is being renewed day by day. For our light affliction, which is but for a moment, is working for us a far more exceeding and eternal weight of glory, while we do not look at the things which are seen, but at the things which are not seen. For the things which are seen are temporary, but the things which are not seen are eternal.
>
> — 2 CORINTHIANS 4:16–18

Our prayer for you today is that you would know the "treasure" and the power of God that is within you.

PERSONAL REFLECTIONS:

- Where are you being hard-pressed?
- How will you overcome today?
- Describe the power of God in you.

DECEMBER 2

What Is Today?

This is the day the LORD has made; we will rejoice and
be glad in it.

— PSALM 118:24

What will today look like for you? Throughout the day, we
all face decisions, obligations, and responsibilities. These
may take us in many directions. However, our priority and
passion to acknowledge our Lord and Savior will be evident
through our deeds and actions.

What day is it? It is the day that the Lord has made. He
has made it holy and has distinguished it from other days.
You will never get another day like it. He has made it for
you; it is, therefore, called the *Lord's day*, for it bears His
image and heart for you.

Whose day will it be? Don't allow the cares of this life to
keep you from praise and worship. Don't allow the influ-

ence of humanism, materialism, and paganism to keep you
from giving glory to God.

> **Our prayer for you today is for you to recognize
> this is the day that the Lord has made so you will
> "rejoice and be glad in it."**

PERSONAL REFLECTIONS:

- What day is it?
- Who will you allow to influence your life today?
- What does the day of the Lord look like to you?

DECEMBER 3

With Whom You Walk Matters

He who walks with wise men will be wise, but the companion of fools will be destroyed.

— PROVERBS 13:20

Who is the "companion of fools"? This is what the Bible says in Psalm 14:1, "The fool hath said in his heart, there is no God. They are corrupt, they have done abominable works, there is none that does good."

The fool is the godless one. Unfortunately, we witness people in our everyday lives who deny God's existence and want nothing to do with the Creator of the heavens and earth. Even worse, they think they are smarter, wiser, and more compassionate than God.

The New Testament describes the way of the fool through the walk of the gentile. For example, in Ephesians 4:17–19, we read,

This I say, therefore, and testify in the Lord, that you should no longer walk as the rest of the Gentiles walk, in the futility of their mind, having their understanding darkened, being alienated from the life of God, because of the ignorance that is in them, because of the blindness of their heart; who, being past feeling, have given themselves over to lewdness, to work all uncleanness with greediness.

Psalm 1:1 tells us there are certain things the blessed and wise person does and does *not* do:

Blessed is the man who walks not in the counsel of the ungodly, nor stands in the path of sinners, nor sits in the seat of the scornful.

The righteous man and the ungodly man are different in how they *think*, how they *behave*, and to whom they *belong*.

The ungodly influence through media, politics, and entertainment, but the righteous man or woman will not walk in it. With all the advice that comes to you from so many different sources, remember the righteous person knows how to stay away from the counsel of the ungodly.

To empower your pursuit of a godly walk, meditate on these three verses:

For all people walk each in the name of his god, but we will walk in the name of the LORD our God forever and ever.

— MICAH 4:5

This is love, that we walk according to His commandments. This is the commandment, that as you have heard from the beginning, you should walk in it.

— 2 JOHN 1:6

As you therefore have received Christ Jesus the Lord, so walk in Him, rooted and built up in Him and established in the faith, as you have been taught, abounding in it with thanksgiving.

— COLOSSIANS 2:6–7

Our prayer for you today is that you simply recognize with whom you walk matters.

PERSONAL REFLECTIONS:

- Who are your companions?
- How will you guard your heart from ungodly influences?
- How will you walk pleasing to the LORD?

DECEMBER 4

Embraced Of God

The burden which the prophet Habakkuk saw.

— HABAKKUK 1:1

Do you have a burden? What the prophet Habakkuk saw burdened him. The prophet cried out against the violence, the lawlessness, and the injustice he saw all around him.

Nations were given to greed, power, idolatry, and immorality. People treated one another inhumanely. Often, it seemed as if power and success came to those who broke God's laws and rejected His legitimate claims as the Creator. Yet, according to Habakkuk, the Lord remains sovereign. He sits in His holy temple watching the earth. He will eventually judge each person for his or her life (2:20).

While people will be seduced into wickedness by the allure of power and success (2:6–20), a glorious future awaits those who submit to God.

Habakkuk was unique among the prophets in that he asked questions of God. The questions he raised were for our sake:

1. Why does evil go unpunished?
2. How can a just God use a wicked nation like Babylon to punish His chosen people?

Habakkuk wanted to know, just as we do, what God was doing and why.

God did not strike Habakkuk down for these questions. He answered them by revealing that the Lord Himself will establish His Kingdom. He will hold all people and nations accountable. The present may be filled with wickedness and chaos, but the future belongs to the righteous.

Our prayer for you today is that you would have the courage to bring your burdens and questions before God, and lay them at His feet.

PERSONAL REFLECTIONS:

- What burden did Habakkuk carry?
- What burden do you carry?
- How will you turn your burden over to God?

DECEMBER 5

All Things Are Possible

Jesus said to him, "If you can believe, all things are possible to him who believes." Immediately the father of the child cried out and said with tears, "Lord, I believe; help my unbelief!"

— MARK 9:23–24

The poor father in this account was challenged by Jesus' exhortation for faith. He did believe in Jesus' power to deliver his boy. After all, why else would he come to Jesus? The fact is he recognized his doubts, so he tearfully pleaded with Jesus: "Lord, I believe; help my unbelief!"

In this case, the man's unbelief was not a rebellion against or a rejection of God's promise. He did not *deny* God's promise; he *desired* it. However, because it was his son and he was so undone, God's promise seemed too good to be true. Therefore, he said, "Help my unbelief!" Here Jesus is teaching us that anything is possible if we believe, because nothing is too difficult for God. This does not mean we can have everything we want, as if by magic, but with faith we can have everything we need to serve and glorify Him.

Sometimes, we can be so preoccupied with problems when we should be looking for opportunities. In other words, instead of focusing on the negative, we should develop an attitude of expectancy. To say God cannot rescue someone from a situation or to say a task is impossible demonstrates a defeated faith.

Our prayer for you today is that you believe all things are possible and remember the truth that says,

And we know that all things work together for good to those who love God, to those who are the called according to *His* purpose.

— ROMANS 8:28

PERSONAL REFLECTIONS:

- Where do you need help believing?
- What seems impossible to you?
- How has God shown His power in your life?

DECEMBER 6

Why Do Nations Rage?

Why do the nations rage, and the people plot a vain thing? The kings of the earth set themselves, and the rulers take counsel together, against the LORD and against His Anointed, saying, "Let us break Their bonds in pieces and cast away Their cords from us."

— PSALM 2:1–3

Why do nations rage? Because the enemy has plans. This enemy is also known as a thief in John 10:10,

"The thief does not come except to steal, and to kill, and to destroy. I have come that they may have life, and that they may have it more abundantly."

So who is this enemy that has plans to come against the LORD and against His anointed? The ultimate enemy is Satan, and to carry out his plans he is raising up wicked leaders who are passionate in their resistance against the holy things of God.

This passion to come against the LORD and His anointed is a hellish and destructive rage against Jesus Christ and His redemptive plan. This antichrist movement is being fought on many battlegrounds: social, political, and religious. It has influenced ideologies, economies, science and medicine, education, music, art, morals, and ethics.

Though these wicked leaders will violently oppose a passionate follower of Jesus Christ, you can take great comfort in this:

> You are of God, little children, and have overcome them, because He who is in you is greater than he who is in the world.
>
> — 1 JOHN 4:4

Our prayer for you can be found in the words of the apostle Paul to young Timothy:

> This charge I commit to you, son Timothy, according to the prophecies previously made concerning you, that by them you may wage the good warfare, having faith and a good conscience, which some having rejected, concerning the faith have suffered shipwreck.
>
> — 1 TIMOTHY 1:18–19

PERSONAL REFLECTIONS:

- Why do the nations rage?
- What is the enemy's plan?
- How will you keep the faith?

DECEMBER 7

Love Is Not Rude

Love ... does not behave rudely.

— 1 CORINTHIANS 13:4–5

Have you ever experienced someone behaving rudely? The verb *rude* conveys the idea of acting disgracefully, contrary, or opposite to proper conduct and decency. Behaving rudely has the meaning of inconsiderate talk, disregard for other people's time or moral conscience, taking advantage of people, tactlessness, ignoring the contributions and ideas of others, and the inappropriate behavior with the opposite sex. In other words, this general disregard for proper social conduct demonstrates a lack of love.

A lack of love was evident in the rude behavior of the church at Corinth. Wealthier members didn't wait for poorer ones to arrive for the Lord's Supper. Instead, they selfishly ate their own expensive foods and left little for the poor to eat (1 Corinthians 11:21–23).

Unfortunately, rude behavior is all around us. Whether it be through politicians, social media, or the entertainment industry, we are inundated by people's rude behavior. Although we may see this as normal for the day and hour in which we live, as followers of Christ we should all agree that being rude has no place in our lives.

Romans 13:10 reminds us, "Love does no harm to a neighbor; therefore love *is* the fulfillment of the law."

And Romans 12:9 says, "*Let* love *be* without hypocrisy. Abhor what is evil. Cling to what is good."

Our prayer for you today is that you would cling to what is good, be faithful to love, and do not behave rudely.

PERSONAL REFLECTIONS:

- Do you need to examine your life for rude behavior?
- How will you stop behaving rudely?
- What does the fulfillment of the law look like?

DECEMBER 8

Blessed Through It All

"But I say to you, love your enemies, bless those who curse you, do good to those who hate you, and pray for those who spitefully use you and persecute you."

— MATTHEW 5:44

The Mosaic law commanded the Israelites to love their neighbor (Leviticus 19:18). Yet some of the teachers in the days of Jesus gave license for hating their enemy. Jesus, however, reminds us that all people are our neighbors, including our enemies. To truly fulfill this law, we must love, bless, do good, and pray for our enemies. In other words, we can't just show love to our friends.

We will all face some kind of opposition and formidable enemy at various seasons in our lives. However, how we treat them reveals the measure of our maturity.

When we live a yielded life to God, we treat people the best regardless of how they treat us. We are not accountable for the actions of others, but we are responsible for our own actions and reactions.

The more we take every circumstance and situation as a golden opportunity to learn and grow, the more the Holy Spirit will teach us truth that will set us free. A life yielded to the Holy Spirit manifests Christ's character and qualities.

Our prayer for you today is that you remain loving no matter what others may say or do to you. Remember the words of Jesus:

Blessed are you when they revile and persecute you, and say all kinds of evil against you falsely for My sake. Rejoice and be exceedingly glad, for great is your reward in heaven, for so they persecuted the prophets who were before you.

— MATTHEW 5:11-12

PERSONAL REFLECTIONS:

- Who is your neighbor?
- How do you treat those who hate you?
- How will you bless, do good to, and love your enemies?

DECEMBER 9

The Watchman's Calling

I have set watchmen on your walls, O Jerusalem; they shall never hold their peace day or night. You who make mention of the LORD, do not keep silent, and give Him no rest till He establishes and till He makes Jerusalem a praise in the earth.

— ISAIAH 62:6–7

Are you a watchman? Watchmen have a constant duty. They are prayer warriors who continually pray, giving God "no rest," yet they are not critics.

Those who understand the significance of the Church realize we have a calling to be a voice of the LORD, to reveal His heart and purpose for our generation. God is raising up a voice that declares His purpose and justice. He will give grace to those who are willing to stand strong in the face of adversity. Those who are called of God are not easily shaken by sudden calamities because of their restful confidence in their Savior and LORD.

God wants us to have full assurance that He is in control of everything in the universe. Regardless of what comes our way, we will not be shaken because our faith is settled in God.

Colossians 2:6–7 reminds us:

> As you therefore have received Christ Jesus the Lord, so walk in Him, rooted and built up in Him and established in the faith, as you have been taught, abounding in it with thanksgiving.

Our prayer for you today is that you would recognize your calling as a watchman. May your confidence in His calling cause you to speak truth and life to your generation.

PERSONAL REFLECTIONS:

- Are you called to be a watchman?
- How would you describe your calling?
- What does it mean to you to "walk in Him"?

DECEMBER 10

Death Vs. Life

For the wages of sin is death, but the gift of God is eternal life in Christ Jesus our Lord.

— ROMANS 6:23

When you work for sin, your wages are death, for death is the byproduct of sin. The good news, however, is we receive the gift of God when we surrender to Him. The key to understanding His gift has everything to do with understanding our condition apart from this gift.

Let's face it, we are not smarter than God. We are not bigger than God. We are not all-knowing like God. The truth is we can't be fruitful without Him. To think otherwise is folly.

The wisdom of the prudent is to understand his way, but the folly of fools is deceit.

— PROVERBS 14:8

What's more, we cannot expect blessings when we are not willing to be directed by God's Word. If we continue to lack discipline and stray from obedience, we will reap a life of chaos and confusion.

We all want blessings, but unless we enter God's ordained plan and yield to the leading of the Holy Spirit, we may find ourselves in dangerous territory.

> And she said, "The Philistines are upon you, Samson!" So he awoke from his sleep, and said, "I will go out as before, at other times, and shake myself free!" But he did not know that the LORD had departed from him.
>
> — JUDGES 16:20

How does someone not know that the LORD has departed from them? Simply put, they have experienced the slow spiritual death that took place as they failed to continue to acknowledge the LORD in all their ways. We are reminded in the Scriptures,

> Trust in the LORD with all your heart, and lean not on your own understanding; in all your ways acknowledge Him, and He shall direct your paths. Do not be wise in your own eyes; fear the LORD and depart from evil.
>
> — PROVERBS 3:5–7

Our prayer for you today is that you will live your life always looking to Christ and obeying His Word

so that you will experience the gift of God, which is eternal life in Him.

PERSONAL REFLECTIONS:

- What are the wages of your sin?
- How do you guard from deception?
- How do you acknowledge the LORD in all your ways?

DECEMBER 11

The Gift Of Repentance

In those days John the Baptist came preaching in the wilderness of Judea, and saying, "Repent, for the kingdom of heaven is at hand!"

— MATTHEW 3:1–2

From that time Jesus began to preach and to say, "Repent, for the kingdom of heaven is at hand."

— MATTHEW 4:17

Repent! It is very unfortunate that some would view the word *repentance* as negative or condemning. The opposite is true. For example, Jesus began His ministry by preaching repentance and, at the same time, shared the heart of the Father in John 3:17–18,

For God did not send His Son into the world to condemn the world, but that the world through Him might be saved. He who believes in Him is not condemned; but he who does not believe is condemned already, because he has not believed in the name of the only begotten Son of God.

Repentance takes humility, and humility will acknowledge sin and the need for a Savior. As 1 John 1:9-10 reminds us,

If we confess our sins [that takes humility], He is faithful and just to forgive us of our sins and to cleanse us from all unrighteousness. If we say that we have not sinned, we make Him a liar, and His word is not in us.

The more submitted to God (humble) we are, the more teachable we will become. The opposite is also true. The more prideful we are, the more unreceptive, unteachable, and unwilling we become. The lack of this humility will ultimately keep us from repentance.

As followers of Christ, we understand that the more we love God, the more we find it less difficult to submit and humble ourselves to the maturing process God is working in us.

By humility and the fear of the LORD are riches and honor and life.

— PROVERBS 22:4

Our prayer for you today is that you would walk in humility and experience the gift of repentance so that times of refreshing would come.

"Repent therefore and be converted, that your sins may be blotted out, so that times of refreshing may come from the presence of the Lord."

— ACTS 3:19

PERSONAL REFLECTIONS:

- How would you describe the word *repent*?
- How do you maintain teachableness?
- Where is humility found in your life?

DECEMBER 12

Wisdom From Above

But the wisdom that is from above is first pure, then peaceable, gentle, willing to yield, full of mercy and good fruits, without partiality and without hypocrisy.

— JAMES 3:17

Do you need wisdom? Receiving wisdom from above enables us to do the right thing in God's sight. This includes doing things with the right spirit, the right motive, the right intent, and the right attitude. When our spirits, motives, intents, and attitudes are right, our actions are right, too.

The more we believers mature, the more we adapt to handling difficulties and solving the challenges that arise in life's journey. When we receive wisdom from above, we are endowed with insight into the root of a problem. Wisdom from above also enables us to solve problems with boldness and grace.

The character of this wisdom is wonderful. It is full of love and a giving heart—consistent with the holiness of God—that bestows mercy and produces good fruit.

Our prayer for you today is that you would have wisdom from above. May you be able to say,

The Lord GOD has given me the tongue of the learned, that I should know how to speak a word in season to him who is weary. He awakens me morning by morning, He awakens my ear to hear as the learned.

— ISAIAH 50:4

PERSONAL REFLECTIONS:

- Do you need wisdom from above?
- How does one gain wisdom in Christ?
- What leads to mercy and good fruit?

DECEMBER 13

Rooted And Grounded In Love

That Christ may dwell in your hearts through faith; that you, being rooted and grounded in love, may be able to comprehend with all the saints what is the width and length and depth and height—to know the love of Christ which passes knowledge; that you may be filled with all the fullness of God.

— EPHESIANS 3:17–19

What does "rooted and grounded in love" look like? Two very important expressions are used to describe how love should be established: "rooted," like a living tree which has deep roots to make it tall and strong; and "grounded," like a building that has deep footers and a firm foundation.

Where we go to help us understand and define how love is established can be the difference between a healthy heart and a damaged heart. When Christ dwells in our hearts, genuine love becomes rooted and grounded in us.

One great chapter in the Bible to help us understand the fullness of God's love is found in 1 Corinthians 13. We discover from reading that chapter that *love is patient and kind.* We also find out what love is not: *Love is not envious, boastful, arrogant, rude, selfish, easily angered, resentful, or joyful in wrongdoing.* And we discover love is an action. *Love rejoices with the truth, bears all things, believes all things, hopes all things, endures all things, and never fails!*

It is very clear in Scripture that love is described by action, not by lofty concepts. The apostle Paul is not writing about how love feels, but rather how it can be seen in action. True love that is rooted and grounded is always demonstrated in action.

Our prayer for you today is that you would be rooted and grounded in genuine love.

PERSONAL REFLECTIONS:

- What does being rooted and grounded look like to you?
- How would you define love?
- What helps you to be rooted and grounded in love?

DECEMBER 14

The Love And Patience Of God

The Lord is not slack concerning His promise, as some count slackness, but is long-suffering toward us, not willing that any should perish but that all should come to repentance.

— 2 PETER 3:9

Because God is love, and love is patient, we understand God is patient. We can all be thankful that the LORD is long-suffering or, in other words, patient and kind.

Have you noticed the Scriptures not only write about individuals' accomplishments but also about their failures? Take Noah for example. Everyone thought he was crazy, but he was also a courageous man of faith and strong will. Against the backdrop of great ridicule, Noah built a huge ark in the middle of the desert because God told him it was going to rain. No one believed him, but the rains did come, and the flood happened. After the water receded, Noah triumphantly left the boat and "got drunk and got naked" (Genesis 9:21).

The Noah most people hear about is fiercely faithful, highly favored, and full of endurance. However, maybe for a flood survivor it was more complicated than we would think, and maybe we need to see that even Noah could have bouts of depression and loneliness.

For those of us who study the Scriptures, we know most biblical characters were a complex mix of strength and weaknesses. David, Abraham, Lot, Saul, Solomon, Rahab, and Sarah were God-loving, brilliant, fearless, loyal, passionate, committed holy men and women. Among the lot were murderers, adulterers, and individuals who battled depression. They could be gentle, holy, defenders of the faith one minute, and insecure, mentally unstable, unbelieving, shrewd, lying, and unforgiving the next.

The good news is *God is patient and kind.* Let's get the message out that Jesus has not given up on people. He is the God of the second chance. He does not judge us based on one season of our lives.

Our prayer for you today is:

Now may the Lord direct your hearts into the love of God and into the patience of Christ.

— 2 THESSALONIANS 3:5

PERSONAL REFLECTIONS:

- What does it mean that love is long-suffering?
- How has God been patient and kind to you?
- What can you do to show the love and patience of God?

DECEMBER 15

The Right Hand Of God

Through the resurrection of Jesus Christ, who has gone into heaven and is at the right hand of God, angels and authorities and powers having been made subject to Him.

— I PETER 3:21–22

Where is Jesus? We are reminded in this passage of Scripture that Jesus "has gone into heaven and is at the right hand of God." We also read "angels and authorities and powers have been made subject to Him."

Being at the "right hand of God" means Christ is in a position of all authority and power. It is for this reason the devil wants to usurp the authority of Jesus Christ. This is why we have cults, atheists, and even world religious leaders who want to rebel against the "right hand of God." All of these attacks against the Word of God are tools of the devil to bring confusion, fear, and unbelief.

Here's the good news: Jesus said the devil and his kingdom don't win in the end,

> And I also say to you that you are Peter, and on this rock I will build My church, and the gates of Hades shall not prevail against it.
>
> — MATTHEW 16:18

We also read these powerful words in Matthew 28:18–19,

> And Jesus came and spoke to them, saying, "All authority has been given to Me in heaven and on earth. Go therefore and make disciples of all the nations, baptizing them in the name of the Father and of the Son and of the Holy Spirit."

Don't worry or fear, God's ultimate plan and purpose will prevail. He alone has *all* authority, and He is at the right hand of God. Just as the psalmist declares in Psalm 145:13:

> Your kingdom is an everlasting kingdom, and Your dominion endures throughout all generations.

Our prayer for you today is that you remember Jesus Christ is at the right hand of God and has all authority.

PERSONAL REFLECTIONS:

- Where is Jesus when you pray?
- Describe what you see when you picture Jesus at the right hand of God in heaven.
- How does the authority of God work in your life?

DECEMBER 16

Useful

All Scripture is God-breathed and is useful for teaching, rebuking, correcting and training in righteousness, so that the servant of God may be thoroughly equipped for every good work.

— 2 TIMOTHY 3:16–17 NIV

Do you ever struggle with feeling useful? The word *useful* is also translated *profitable* or *beneficial*. Most of us want to have purpose or to be useful—to be a blessing and not a curse. In other words, we want to be valuable and beneficial to others. Yet, we face three major influences in our lives.

- The secular world (which is being influenced by humanism, agnosticism, and atheism);
- Our broken-down flesh (the Bible calls it the "lust of the flesh, the lust of our eyes, and the pride of life" in 1 John 2:16);

- The devil, who wants to kill, steal, and destroy.

Here is the good news: *As long as we have the Scriptures in our hearts, we have value and are useful and beneficial.*

For example, one of my favorite verses says,

> And now these three remain: faith, hope and love. But the greatest of these is love.
>
>   — 1 CORINTHIANS 13:13

We are reminded in this verse that faith, hope, and love abide and remain.

Faith is valuable and worth fighting for:

> Fight the good fight of faith, lay hold on eternal life, to which you were also called and have confessed the good confession in the presence of many witnesses.
>
>   — 1 TIMOTHY 6:12

Hope is valuable and worth living for:

> Blessed be the God and Father of our Lord Jesus Christ, who according to His abundant mercy has begotten us again to a living hope through the resurrection of Jesus Christ from the dead.
>
>   — 1 PETER 1:3

Love is the greatest of all. It gives purpose and meaning to life:

> Beloved, let us love one another, for love is of God; and everyone who loves is born of God and knows God. He who does not love does not know God, for God is love. In this the love of God was manifested toward us, that God has sent His only begotten Son into the world, that we might live through Him. In this is love, not that we loved God, but that He loved us and sent His Son to be the propitiation for our sins. Beloved, if God so loved us, we also ought to love one another.
>
> — 1 JOHN 4:7–11

Our prayer is that you would be encouraged and remember that, with the Scriptures in your heart, you have what is useful and profitable.

PERSONAL REFLECTIONS:

- What does it mean to you to be useful?
- What value do you place on the Word of God?
- If we "ought to love one another," how do we do it?

DECEMBER 17

Loved By The Father

"He who has My commandments and keeps them, it is he who loves Me. And he who loves Me will be loved by My Father, and I will love him and manifest Myself to him."

— JOHN 14:21

Do you love the Son of God, the Messiah, Jesus Christ? If you do, you love keeping His commands. As Jesus said in John 14:23-24,

If anyone loves Me, he will keep My word; and My Father will love him, and We will come to him and make Our home with him. He who does not love Me does not keep My words; and the word which you hear is not Mine but the Father's who sent Me.

In the natural, as parents, if you are good to our children, you are good to us. In other words, if you are good to our children, we love you. Spiritually speaking, if you love the Son of God (Jesus), the Father loves you.

Consider the magnitude of Jesus' promise: If we persevere in love and obedience, Jesus progressively will reveal Himself to us. Jesus said His followers show their love for Him by trusting and obeying Him. Love is more than just words. It's demonstrated in our commitment, conduct, and loyalty. If we love Christ, then we must live by trusting and obeying what He says in His Word.

Here's the good news: *Jesus saves the deepest revelation of Himself for those who love and serve Him.*

Our prayer for you today is that you would have His commandments in your heart. Let it be your testimony that you desire to love, obey, and honor Him in everything you do today.

PERSONAL REFLECTIONS:

- How do you have His commandments in your heart?
- How do you know that God loves you?
- What is your testimony of His love?

DECEMBER 18

Give Thanks

O, give thanks unto the LORD, for He is good: for His mercy endureth for ever.

— PSALM 107:1 KJV

Do you sometimes struggle to give thanks? We want to remind you today that giving thanks is more than just a good idea: It's like blood flowing in your life. In the natural, if your blood stops flowing, eventually your heart will stop beating. In our spiritual lives, if we no longer have a thankful heart, then our purpose in life becomes lifeless or lost.

There's a strong warning in Romans 1:21:

Because, although they knew God, they did not glorify Him as God, nor were thankful, but became futile in their thoughts, and their foolish hearts were darkened.

The apostle Paul also admonishes us:

> In everything give thanks; for this is the will of God in
> Christ Jesus for you.

>   — 1 THESSALONIANS 5:18

And in Ephesians 5:20, he said,

> Giving thanks always for all things to God the Father in
> the name of our Lord Jesus Christ.

We ought always to give thanks *in everything* because we
recognize God's sovereignty—His hand and His grace
seeing us through.

**Our prayer for you today is that you would fulfill
the will of God by giving Him thanks in all things.**

PERSONAL REFLECTIONS:

- What hinders you from giving thanks?
- What reminds you to give thanks?
- How do you give thanks "always for all things"?

DECEMBER 19

Think Soberly

For I say, through the grace given to me, to everyone who is among you, not to think of himself more highly than he ought to think, but to think soberly, as God has dealt to each one a measure of faith.

— ROMANS 12:3

How do we keep from pride and arrogance? The key is remembering His grace has been extended to us. This is why the apostle Paul admonishes us not to think of ourselves more highly than we ought to think. We're to "think soberly."

What does it mean to "think soberly"? The Greek word *so-fro-ne'-o* translated *soberly* means:

1. To be of sound mind
2. To be in one's right mind
3. To exercise self-control

Our focus needs to be on the LORD who gives grace to live. "God has dealt to each one a measure of faith," our opening verse tells us. What this communicates is that we have no basis for pride. We ought not to have a superior opinion of ourselves, for as James 1:17 says,

> Every good gift and every perfect gift is from above, and comes down from the Father of lights, with whom there is no variation or shadow of turning.

The sad truth is pride and arrogance keep us from thinking soberly of ourselves. This pride also makes us blind to our own faults and critical of the faults of others. Even worse, pride thinks, *I don't need God!*

The Bible is very clear that the person who thinks too highly of himself fools and deceives himself beyond repair (Galatians 6:3). However, when we see ourselves as we really are, and we see Him as He really is, we won't be given over to pride.

As followers of Christ—when we live the truth, speak the truth, and think the truth—we are kept from deception and insincere living.

Our prayer for you today is that you would think soberly, reminding yourself of the gift of His grace.

PERSONAL REFLECTIONS:

- How has grace been given to you?
- What does it mean to you to think soberly?
- How do you guard your heart from deception?

DECEMBER 20

He Who Promised Is Faithful

Let us hold fast the confession of our hope without wavering, for He who promised is faithful.

— HEBREWS 10:23

Discouragement can make many waver from the truth. A renewed confidence in the hope of Jesus makes us stand strong in the faith. Hope is worth holding onto. Hope is also something we are called to confess. Another translation talks about keeping hope secure.

How do we hold fast to this hope? The key is found in believing "He who promised is faithful." Faith in the promises of God will carry us through whatever this world throws at us. It is far better to trust in His faithfulness than our own abilities!

We can take great courage knowing God never intended for us to walk in our own strength and power. This is why we can rejoice knowing, "He who calls you is faithful, who also will do it."

Sanctification is God's work in us. It's a testament to His faithfulness. Paul said in Ephesians 5:25–27:

> Husbands, love your wives, just as Christ also loved the church and gave Himself for her, that He might sanctify and cleanse her with the washing of water by the word, that He might present her to Himself a glorious church, not having spot or wrinkle or any such thing, but that she should be holy and without blemish.

Our prayer for you today is that you hold fast the confession of your hope, knowing He is faithful.

> Now may the God of peace Himself sanctify you completely; and may your whole spirit, soul, and body be preserved blameless at the coming of our Lord Jesus Christ. He who calls you *is* faithful, who also will do *it*.

— 1 THESSALONIANS 5:23–24

PERSONAL REFLECTIONS:

- How do you hold fast to the confession of your hope?
- Have you ever struggled seeing His faithfulness?
- How has God shown Himself faithful to you?

DECEMBER 21

Following My Example

Brethren, join in following my example, and note those who so walk, as you have us for a pattern.

— PHILIPPIANS 3:17

"Follow my example!" Have you every made such a bold statement to someone? We shouldn't think the apostle Paul was being egotistical here. He knew he was not a sinless or perfect example, yet he still could tell the Philippians to follow his example. He told the Corinthians to do the same:

Imitate me, just as I also *imitate* Christ.

— 1 CORINTHIANS 11:1

Paul's life was an example of a life devoted to following Christ in humility. You can't be an example if you lack humility and self-discipline because it will lead to weak character. And weak character opens the door to defeat and destruction, for yourself and for those who follow you. In other words, a potential leader who neglects humility and self-discipline, due to an inflated ego and a high position, ends up missing God's heart and destroying his or her effectiveness. This is one of the reasons Paul told Timothy,

> Let no one despise your youth, but be an example to the believers in word, in conduct, in love, in spirit, in faith, in purity.
>
> — 1 TIMOTHY 4:12

Be an example by what you say (word), what you do (conduct), and how you do it (love and purity).

Our prayer for you today is that you will live in such a way that others can see the love of Christ working in and through you.

PERSONAL REFLECTIONS:

- Is it hard for you to say, "Follow my example"?
- Can you recall a time when someone imitated you?
- How is God speaking to you today?

DECEMBER 22

Endure Suffering With Focus

Endure suffering along with me, as a good soldier of Christ Jesus. Soldiers don't get tied up in the affairs of civilian life, for then they cannot please the officer who enlisted them. And athletes cannot win the prize unless they follow the rules. And hardworking farmers should be the first to enjoy the fruit of their labor. Think about what I am saying. The Lord will help you understand all these things.

— 2 TIMOTHY 2:3–7 NLT

Do you enjoy suffering? Don't answer that. Who ever enjoys suffering?

In the natural, muscles are developed by training, not by wishful thinking. And in the natural, all soldiers, athletes, and farmers need to be willing to pay the price of self-discipline and self-denial to be successful.

In the same way, if believers are not willing to endure hardship, they will never accomplish much for Jesus Christ. If they give up as soon as something hard is put before them, they cannot fulfill Jesus' call:

> If anyone desires to come after Me, let him deny himself, and take up his cross, and follow Me.
>
> — MATTHEW 16:24

Sometimes, we can make up our own rules for our Christian life as if that's okay. For some people, their special arrangement goes something like this: "I know this is sin, but God understands, so I'll just keep doing it and asking Him to forgive me later." This goes against the attitude of an athlete who must compete according to the rules.

Let us encourage you with this: You don't have to enjoy suffering; you just need to endure it with the strength of the LORD. And with His strength, you will experience grace that will enable you to see beyond the present trial.

Our prayer for you today is that you would be able to speak the words of 1 Peter 4:12–13:

> Beloved, do not think it strange concerning the fiery trial which is to try you, as though some strange thing happened to you; but rejoice to the extent that you partake of Christ's sufferings, that when His glory is revealed, you may also be glad with exceeding joy.

PERSONAL REFLECTIONS:

- What is God calling you to endure?
- Do you find it difficult to deny yourself, take up your cross, and follow Him? Why?
- How do you receive His strength to endure?

DECEMBER 23

Missing Key

"I am He who lives, and was dead, and behold, I am alive forevermore. Amen. And I have the keys of Hades and of Death."

— REVELATION 1:18

The date was April 15, 1912. It is a date that will live forever in the history of our country and of our world because that was the day the *Titanic* sank. Most people know the *Titanic* ran into an iceberg as it made its maiden voyage from South Hampton England to the United States. But not many people know that it was the second reason the *Titanic* sank. The first reason the *Titanic* sank was because of a "missing key."

On the day before its launch, David Blair, the second officer of the ship, was reassigned. David Blair had in his pocket the key to the "crow's nest locker." Inside the crow's nest locker were binoculars. These binoculars were used by the person who would be in the crow's nest as lookout. And because David Blair had mistakenly taken the key to the crow's nest locker, the binoculars were not available. So the lookout in the crow's nest was only able to see with his human sight. He didn't see the iceberg. The iceberg was the second reason for this great devastation that resulted the death of over 1,500 people.

The Scriptures remind us that Jesus is the One who has "the keys of Hades and of Death." Some think the devil is the one with authority over hell and the power to determine life or death. Clearly, they are wrong, for Jesus said,

> And do not fear those who kill the body but cannot kill the soul. But rather fear Him who is able to destroy both soul and body in hell.
>
> — MATTHEW 10:28

In other words, we can trust Jesus will never let the devil take the keys, for only He holds the keys.

Our prayer for you today is that you would remember the importance of Jesus' words to His disciples from Matthew 16:19:

And I will give you the keys of the kingdom of heaven, and whatever you bind on earth will be bound in heaven, and whatever you loose on earth will be loosed in heaven.

PERSONAL REFLECTIONS:

- Have you ever lost something? How did it make you feel?
- Have you every felt like the enemy had the keys of authority?
- What does Jesus mean by "the keys of the kingdom of heaven"?

DECEMBER 24

Confessing The Prince Of Peace

For unto us a Child is born, unto us a Son is given; and the government will be upon His shoulder. And His name will be called Wonderful, Counselor, Mighty God, Everlasting Father, Prince of Peace.

— ISAIAH 9:6

Jesus Christ has come in the flesh. This glorious prophecy of the birth of the Messiah in Isaiah reminds Israel that the Messiah would be a man. This Child would be a man, but more than a man. He is also the eternal Son of God. That Jesus is both God and man tells us that man really is made in the image of God (Genesis 1:26).

If Jesus were not fully man, He could not stand in the place of sinful man and be a substitute for the punishment man deserves. If He were not fully God, His sacrifice would be insufficient. If Jesus is not fully God and fully man, we are left with the conclusion that we are lost in sin. Sin is what keeps the world from peace.

> And suddenly there was with the angel a multitude of the heavenly host praising God and saying: "Glory to God in the highest, And on earth peace, goodwill toward men!"
>
> — LUKE 2:13–14

We read in this verse that the "heavenly host" proclaimed *peace*. The world needed that peace then, and the world needs it today. However, peace can only come to the earth when the *Prince of Peace* is recognized and acknowledged as the *Son* who *is given*.

I've heard it said, "Let God have all the glory, so we may have the peace."

Our prayer for you today is may:

> "The LORD bless you and keep you; the LORD make His face shine upon you, and be gracious to you; the LORD lift up His countenance upon you, and give you peace."
>
> — NUMBERS 6:24–26

PERSONAL REFLECTIONS:

- How do you celebrate the birth of Christ?
- Do you struggle with knowing His peace at times?
- What does peace look like to you?

DECEMBER 25

The Birth Of Jesus

And it came to pass in those days that a decree went out from Caesar Augustus that all the world should be registered.... So all went to be registered, everyone to his own city. Joseph also went up from Galilee, out of the city of Nazareth, into Judea, to the city of David, which is called Bethlehem, because he was of the house and lineage of David, to be registered with Mary, his betrothed wife, who was with child. So it was, that while they were there, the days were completed for her to be delivered. And she brought forth her firstborn Son, and wrapped Him in swaddling cloths, and laid Him in a manger, because there was no room for them in the inn.

— LUKE 2:1–7

Have you ever been promised a gift but didn't receive it? It's a real let down, isn't it? Most of us have experienced that disappointment at some point in our lives. When we read the story of Jesus' birth, we find great hope in knowing God keeps His promises.

Through the prophets, God had promised Israel that a Savior would come. The prophets declared what the Savior would do, and all the things they said about Jesus' birth came to pass.

Mary gave birth to Jesus in the town of Bethlehem—an ordinary, quiet place. However, this little town became a spectacular place because of the birth of Christ. That night in Bethlehem (also known as *the place of bread*), God came down to Earth in the form of a little baby. God gave Jesus a humble beginning so that everyone could understand He came to bring salvation to all people, even the poorest and lowliest.

The stable Jesus was born in may have been a cave located behind an inn. Many believe it was where the Levitical shepherds raised the sacrificial lambs that, when birthed, were wrapped in cloths. It's a beautiful picture when you think how Bethlehem (a place of bread), the cave (a place for sacrificial lambs), and the manger (a place for feeding) all symbolize what Christ became for the world.

It truly is a Merry Christmas when we know the real meaning of Christmas, and it's very special knowing He keeps His promises.

Our prayer for you today is that you would have a Christ-filled day, knowing His promises are true.

PERSONAL REFLECTIONS:

- What has been one of your greatest gifts in life?
- What does the birth of Jesus remind you of?
- How will you share His promises with others?

DECEMBER 26

Without Me, You Can Do Nothing

"Abide in Me, and I in you. As the branch cannot bear fruit of itself, unless it abides in the vine, neither can you, unless you abide in Me. I am the vine, you are the branches. He who abides in Me, and I in him, bears much fruit; for without Me you can do nothing."

— JOHN 15:4-5

What can you do without God? With the New Year approaching, people will be making all kinds of New Year's resolutions, starting new goals, and creating new projects. Being task- or goal-oriented is not all bad, but the problem comes when we forget the Source of our strength.

When Jesus said, "Without Me you can do nothing," it wasn't as if the disciples could do no *activity* without Jesus. They could be active without Him. Yet, they and we can do nothing of real, eternal value without Jesus. Jesus emphasized a *mutual* relationship. The disciples not only abide in the Master; the Master also abides in the disciples:

I am my beloved's, and my beloved is mine.

— SONG OF SOLOMON 6:3

When Jesus says, "Abide in Me," He is talking about the will, the choices, and the decisions we make. We must decide to do things which join ourselves to Him and keep ourselves in contact with Him. This is what it means to abide in Jesus.

Our prayer for you today is that you would "abide" in the One who will make your paths righteous and full of blessings.

He restores my soul; He leads me in the path of righteousness for His name's sake.

— PSALM 23:3

PERSONAL REFLECTIONS:

- What are some of your goals for the coming year?
- Have you recently tried to do things without God and failed?
- What does it mean to abide?

DECEMBER 27

The Danger And Destruction Of Coveting

For this you know, that no fornicator, unclean person, nor covetous man, who is an idolater, has any inheritance in the kingdom of Christ and God. Let no one deceive you with empty words, for because of these things the wrath of God comes upon the sons of disobedience.

— EPHESIANS 5:5–6

Why is coveting so dangerous? Because it ultimately keeps an individual from inheriting the kingdom of God. Covetousness avoids discipline, diligence, and character. According to its biblical usage, a covetous person is:

1. Eager to have more, especially wanting what belongs to others.
2. Greedy of gain, covetous.

No individual will ever excel by coveting, but rather by diligent study and focused discipline. If potential leaders covet position, prestige, or money, they will destroy their fruitfulness in life. When leaders forget who the Giver of gifts is, they become deceived.

Remember there are no shortcuts to character.

Our prayer is that you would discern the dangers of covetousness and run diligently toward the Father of lights.

Do not be deceived, my beloved brethren. Every good gift and every perfect gift is from above, and comes down from the Father of lights, with whom there is no variation or shadow of turning. Of His own will He brought us forth by the word of truth, that we might be a kind of firstfruits of His creatures.

— JAMES 1:16–18

PERSONAL REFLECTIONS:

- How would you define the dangers of coveting?
- Have you witnessed a life destroyed by coveting?
- How do you avoid coveting?

DECEMBER 28

By Whose Stripes We Are Healed

Who has believed our report? And to whom has the arm of the LORD been revealed? For He shall grow up before Him as a tender plant, and as a root out of dry ground. He has no form or comeliness; and when we see Him, there is no beauty that we should desire Him. He is despised and rejected by men, a man of sorrows and acquainted with grief. And we hid, as it were, our faces from Him; He was despised, and we did not esteem Him. Surely He has borne our griefs and carried our sorrows; yet we esteemed Him stricken, smitten by God, and afflicted. But He was wounded for our transgressions, He was bruised for our iniquities; the chastisement for our peace was upon Him, and by His stripes we are healed.

— ISAIAH 53:1-5

Ultimate *wholeness* and *healing* are based on knowing who this passage is talking about. People are searching for wholeness and healing, but without receiving them from the true Source, wholeness and healing are temporary or nonexistent.

There has been much debate as to if the prophet Isaiah had spiritual healing or physical healing in mind. As these scriptures are quoted in the New Testament, we gain further insights.

Mathew 8:16–17 seems to address physical healing. First Peter 2:24–25 seems to deal with spiritual healing. We can safely conclude God has both aspects of healing in mind, and both are provided for by the suffering of the Messiah– the LORD Jesus Christ.

Further study will reveal the Bible says we *have been saved* (Ephesians 2:8), *are being saved* (1 Corinthians 1:18), and *will be saved* (1 Corinthians 3:15). Even so, there is a sense in which we have been healed, are being healed, and one day will be healed and whole.

God's ultimate healing is called *resurrection*, and it is a glorious promise to every follower of Jesus Christ.

> But now Christ is risen from the dead, *and* has become the firstfruits of those who have fallen asleep. For since by man *came* death, by Man also *came* the resurrection of the dead. For as in Adam all die, even so in Christ all shall be made alive.
>
> — 1 CORINTHIANS 15:20–22

Our prayer for you today is that you would know His provision of wholeness and healing.

Beloved, I pray that you may prosper in all things and be in health, just as your soul prospers.

— 3 JOHN 1:2

PERSONAL REFLECTIONS:

- Where does healing come from?
- How would you describe healing?
- What is more important—physical or spiritual healing?

DECEMBER 29

In The Last Days

Therefore, since Christ suffered for us in the flesh, arm yourselves also with the same mind, for he who has suffered in the flesh has ceased from sin.... In regard to these, they think it strange that you do not run with them in the same flood of dissipation, speaking evil of you.... But the end of all things is at hand; therefore be serious and watchful in your prayers. And above all things have fervent love for one another, for "love will cover a multitude of sins." Be hospitable to one another without grumbling. As each one has received a gift, minister it to one another, as good stewards of the manifold grace of God."

— I PETER 4:1–10

Are we in the last days? Many have debated this question for decades. Whether you believe we are or not shouldn't keep you from believing we are living in dangerous times.

The apostle Peter is giving some strong warnings in our opening passage. Serving God in the last days is going to take courage and clear thinking. Our attitudes are going to be tested. We need to keep the focus to fight the good fight of faith.

In the last days,

1. Christians should have an attitude of commitment to the will of God (1 Peter 4:1–3).
2. Christians should live with an attitude of wisdom (1 Peter 4:4–6).
3. Christians should live with an attitude of serious prayer (1 Peter 4:7).
4. Christians should live with an attitude of love (1 Peter 4:8–11).

If we really believe we are living in the last days, it is all the more appropriate we give ourselves to these four attitudes.

Remember, as believers, we are told to give ourselves to serious and watchful prayer, primarily having our hearts and minds ready for the return of Jesus Christ.

Our prayer for you today is that you would maintain an attitude that is pleasing to your heavenly Father in these last days.

PERSONAL REFLECTIONS:

- Do you believe we are living in the last days?
- How would you define the last days?
- What are you doing to prepare for the coming of the LORD?

DECEMBER 30

Delivered From All Fears

I sought the LORD, and He heard me, and delivered me from all my fears.

— PSALM 34:4

Have you ever battled fear? It's very real in all of our lives, but those who learn to cry out to the LORD find deliverance.

The definition of the Hebrew word that's translated *sought* in our opening verse is:

A primitive root; properly, to tread or frequent; usually to follow (for pursuit or search); by implication, to seek or ask, specifically to worship; inquire, make inquisition, require, search, seek (for, out).

— STRONG'S EXHAUSTIVE
CONCORDANCE

Notice how the word has a continual or frequent meaning. In other words, it is not a one time thing. In the New Testament, we have a Greek word translated *seek* that has the same concept. For example, in Matthew 6:33, we read:

> "But seek first the kingdom of God and His righteousness, and all these things shall be added to you."

Seek, in this sense, implies ongoing worship. So, in our opening verse when the psalmist said, "I sought the LORD," he was describing a pattern in life. When he continued to seek the LORD, he experienced deliverance. This was no ordinary deliverance. This deliverance had to do with being delivered from *all* fears. David's continued prayers helped to silence all his fears.

Our prayer for you today is that you would experience deliverance from all of your fears as you continue to seek Him.

PERSONAL REFLECTIONS:

- What are you afraid of?
- What does it mean to seek the LORD?
- What does deliverance look like to you?

DECEMBER 31

According To The Will Of God

Therefore let those who suffer according to the will of God commit their souls to Him in doing good, as to a faithful Creator.

— 1 PETER 4:19

Suffering is not a topic we like to talk about. However, anyone who spends time in the Bible will not be able to deny the reality of its truth. For example, when we consider the life of John the Baptist and how his life ended, we realize suffering is very real for the disciples of Christ.

So he sent and had John beheaded in prison. And his head was brought on a platter and given to the girl, and she brought it to her mother. Then his disciples came and took away the body and buried it, and went and told Jesus.

— MATTHEW 14:10-12

Maybe we won't experience the suffering of imprisonment and beheading, but neither will we get a free pass on suffering. This is what we read in 2 Timothy 3:12:

> Yes, and all who desire to live godly in Christ Jesus will suffer persecution.

The question is not *if* we face suffering, but when we do, how will we endure it? Look at our opening verse again. The key is to *commit your soul in doing good*. Ultimately, our commitment is acknowleging that God is the faithful Creator who has an eternal plan. Therefore remember this:

> For I consider that the sufferings of this present time are not worthy to be compared with the glory which shall be revealed in us.
>
> — ROMANS 8:18

Our prayer for you today is that you would commit your soul to Him in doing good, no matter the cost, according to the will of God.

But may the God of all grace, who called us to His eternal glory by Christ Jesus, after you have suffered a while, perfect, establish, strengthen, and settle you.

> — 1 PETER 5:10

PERSONAL REFLECTIONS:

- How would you describe suffering?
- What does it mean to you that all who desire to live godly in Christ Jesus will suffer persecution?
- Can you describe the glory which shall be revealed?

JANUARY 1

Wait On The LORD

I would have lost heart, unless I had believed that I would see the goodness of the LORD in the land of the living. Wait on the LORD; be of good courage, and He shall strengthen your heart; wait, I say, on the LORD!

— PSALM 27:13-14

Do you like waiting? When we are in a crisis, or a difficult season of life, it can be challenging to wait on the LORD for an answer.

Waiting for God can seem as if God isn't answering or doesn't understand the urgency of the hour. However, that kind of thinking can lead to our feeling like God is not in control or possibly He is unjust. Truthfully, this type of attack in our minds can be a subtle attempt of the devil to keep us from seeking God for courage and strength. It is vital that we understand God is worth waiting for.

"The LORD *is* my portion," says my soul, therefore I hope in Him! The LORD *is* good to those who wait for Him, to the soul *who* seeks Him. *It is* good that *one* should hope and wait quietly For the salvation of the LORD.

— LAMENTATIONS 3:24–26

We need to be reminded that God often uses waiting on Him to refresh, renew, and strengthen our hearts. Let us make good use of seasons of waiting on Him by discovering how God is working more of His character in and through us.

Our prayer for you today is that you would learn to wait upon the LORD.

But those who wait on the LORD shall renew *their* strength; they shall mount up with wings like eagles, they shall run and not be weary, they shall walk and not faint.

— ISAIAH 40:31

PERSONAL REFLECTIONS:

- How do you deal with waiting?
- What does it mean to wait on the LORD?
- Why is our attitude during a season of waiting important?

JANUARY 2

Not Forsaking The Assembly

And let us consider one another in order to stir up love and good works, not forsaking the assembling of ourselves together, as is the manner of some, but exhorting one another, and so much the more as you see the Day approaching.

— HEBREWS 10:24–25

Do you like going to your local church? The Scriptures exhort us that as we see *the Day* of Jesus' return approaching, we should be *more* committed to the fellowship of God's people, the *assembling of ourselves together*.

Many go to their local church if they feel they "need it" at the time. But our motivation for fellowship needs to take on a greater meaning. Ultimately, we should obey God by giving to others. In other words, we should all be gathering for fellowship and looking for opportunities to share our gifts with others.

We must beware of those who seem to be so "spiritual" that they can't get along with others in any local church. These are people who seem to be so gifted, so prophetic, or so spiritual that they get kicked out or leave in a huff from every church they go to. Being like this is not being Christlike. Eventually, they are isolated from healthy fellowship.

Forsaking fellowship is also a sure way to give place to discouragement. When we avoid fellowship, we remove ourselves from a place where God's people encourage each other in the Faith.

Our prayer for you today is:

How is it then, brethren? Whenever you come together, each of you has a psalm, has a teaching, has a tongue, has a revelation, has an interpretation. Let all things be done for edification.

— 1 CORINTHIANS 14:26

PERSONAL REFLECTIONS:

- How important is the local church to you?
- What does real fellowship look like?
- Do you go to your local church with expectancy?

JANUARY 3

The Spirit Of The Antichrist

Beloved, do not believe every spirit, but test the spirits, whether they are of God; because many false prophets have gone out into the world. By this you know the Spirit of God: Every spirit that confesses that Jesus Christ has come in the flesh is of God, and every spirit that does not confess that Jesus Christ has come in the flesh is not of God. And this is the spirit of the Antichrist, which you have heard was coming, and is now already in the world.

— 1 JOHN 4:1–3

Today, some groups deny that Jesus is God (such as the Jehovah's Witnesses, Mormons, and Muslims). During the time of Jesus' ministry on Earth, people didn't have a hard time believing He was God. What they actually had a hard time believing was that He was a *real* man. This false teaching said Jesus was truly God (which is correct) and really a "make-believe" man (which is incorrect).

Who is a liar but he who denies that Jesus is the Christ?
He is antichrist who denies the Father and the Son.

— 1 JOHN 2:22

The context in 1 John makes it clear that to affirm Jesus is
the Christ is more than just saying, "He is the Messiah." It
has to do with understanding the relationship between
Jesus and God the Father. In other words, someone could
say, "I believe Jesus is the Christ as I define *Christ*." But we
must believe that Jesus is the Christ as the Bible defines
Christ—the Messiah, who is fully God and fully man and
who perfectly revealed the Father to us.

**Our prayer for you today is that you would believe
what Jesus said,**

He who believes in Me, believes not in Me but in Him
who sent Me. And he who sees Me sees Him who
sent Me.

— JOHN 12:44-45

He who receives Me receives Him who sent Me.

— JOHN 13:20

PERSONAL REFLECTIONS:

- Who is Jesus?
- Who will influence your life today?
- What does the Day of the LORD look like to you?

JANUARY 4

Ask, Seek, Knock

"Ask, and it will be given to you; seek, and you will find; knock, and it will be opened to you. For everyone who asks receives, and he who seeks finds, and to him who knocks it will be opened. Or what man is there among you who, if his son asks for bread, will give him a stone? Or if he asks for a fish, will he give him a serpent? If you then, being evil, know how to give good gifts to your children, how much more will your Father who is in heaven give good things to those who ask Him!"

— MATTHEW 7:7–11

What are you asking God for? Some people seek God earnestly only when they are in trouble, but the beauty of spending time in the Word of God daily is that we seek Him intensely all the time.

Ask—seek—knock. We see a progressive intensity going

from ask to seek to knock. Jesus told us to have intensity, passion, and persistence in our relationship with Him.

I've heard it said, "*Ask* with confidence and humility. *Seek* with care and application. *Knock* with earnestness and perseverance." The idea of knocking also implies that we sense resistance. After all, if the door were already open, there would be no need to knock. Yet Jesus encourages us that, even if we sense the door is closed and we must knock, then we do so and continue to do so daily, and we will see the answer.

Our prayer for you today is that you would

Seek the Lord and His strength; seek His face evermore!

— PSALM 105:4

PERSONAL REFLECTIONS:

- What are you asking of the Father?
- What does seeking the LORD mean to you?
- How do you knock at His door?

JANUARY 5

True Riches

To me, who am less than the least of all the saints, this grace was given, that I should preach among the Gentiles the unsearchable *riches* of Christ.

— EPHESIANS 3:8

What do true riches look like to you? We know people all over the world are seeking riches. Unfortunately, many people are being confused or deceived about what true riches are. There are many reasons for which people seek riches—for confidence, power, and peace—but in the end they become disappointed.

The apostle Paul is reminding the Ephesian church that this mystery is like great riches for the gentiles. They can now stand before the LORD in a way they could only dream of before. Paul himself marveled at the grace given to him by which he was called to preach the gospel that reveals the mystery. When we consider Paul's personal story, we see his calling really was all about God's grace.

The redemption and forgiveness given to us come according to the measure of the riches of His grace. It is not a *small* redemption or forgiveness won by Jesus on the cross. It is *huge*!

Trying to measure the greatness of God's grace is like trying to measure out the shore of a lake that you discover is not a lake at all but an ocean, an immeasurable sea. God's riches are "unsearchable" and beyond what we can imagine or think. Throughout eternity, we will worship God with His unsearchable riches.

Our prayer for you today is that

He might make known the riches of His glory on the vessels of mercy, which He had prepared beforehand for glory.

— ROMANS 9:23

PERSONAL REFLECTIONS:

- How would you describe true riches?
- Why are the riches of Christ unsearchable?
- When did you first experience the riches of His grace?

JANUARY 6

Filled With Joy And The Holy Spirit

And the disciples were filled with joy and with the Holy Spirit.

— ACTS 13:52

Are you filled with joy *and* the Holy Spirit? We have to admit that it's possible for people to live out their lives and yet have an unproductive spiritual life. The problem comes when church goers and synagogue attendees never:

1. Respond to the call to *go* and make disciples.
2. See anything supernatural happen in answer to their prayers.
3. Experience freedom from lingering habits and addictive patterns.
4. Sense the explosive release of the Holy Spirit's passion for the broken.
5. Feel the rush of the peace, joy, and strength that comes from His presence.

God's purpose for our lives involves so much more. He wants us to experience His joy and the power of the Holy Spirit. This generation and our children's generation need to be a part of personally:

1. Leading hundreds of people to faith in Christ.
2. Praying and witnessing the power of God to heal and deliver people.
3. Experiencing His love, joy, and peace in the midst of a world in chaos and confusion.

Our prayer for you today is that you would hunger for more of God's love, joy, and peace flowing in and through your life.

Now may the God of hope fill you with all joy and peace believing, that you may abound in hope by the power of the Holy Spirit.

— ROMANS 15:13

PERSONAL REFLECTIONS:

- What does it mean to be filled with joy and the Holy Spirit?
- What is God's purpose for your life?
- How do you maintain the joy of the Lord?

JANUARY 7

Communication

Death and life are in the power of the tongue, and those who love it will eat its fruit.

— PROVERBS 18:21

Do you work on communication? Most of us will have the opportunity to speak and/or write words today. What we speak and write will have consequences. What we speak and write will build up others or tear them down. What we speak will bless or curse because "death and life are in the power of the tongue."

The tongue not only has the power of provision, but also the power of death and life. As followers of Jesus Christ, we need to know how to watch our tongue, speaking only what is good for necessary edification, desiring to impart grace to all who hear us. Ephesians 4:29 says,

Let no corrupt word proceed out of your mouth, but what is good for necessary edification, that it may impart grace to the hearers.

We followers of Christ need to show the same kindness, tenderheartedness, and forgiveness to others that God shows us. If we treat others as God treats us, we fulfill the Word of God:

And be kind to one another, tenderhearted, forgiving one another, even as God in Christ forgave you.

— EPHESIANS 4:32

Our prayer for you today is that you would be used by God to speak life, speak encouragement, and speak blessings.

PERSONAL REFLECTIONS:

- Do you see the need to work on your communication?
- What is "good for necessary edification"?
- How do you speak life and not death?

JANUARY 8

Rejoice With Those Who Rejoice, And Weep With Those Who Weep

Rejoicing in hope, patient in tribulation, continuing steadfastly in prayer; distributing to the needs of the saints, given to hospitality. Bless those who persecute you; bless and do not curse. Rejoice with those who rejoice, and weep with those who weep.

— ROMANS 12:12–15

Do you like rejoicing with those who are rejoicing? When we take a look at the news around us, we see the suffering, pain, and discouragement in our society. For example, the story of tornadoes in Alabama a few years ago that caused the death of over 24 people is heartbreaking. It can be overwhelming to think of the devastation people go through every day.

That being said, however, difficult times do not mean we should abandon hope, patience, or continuing steadfastly in prayer. Trials do not excuse a lack of love in the Body of Christ or a lack of willingness to do His work.

"Rejoice with those who rejoice, and weep with those who weep" is a simple reminder to be considerate of the feelings of others. Genuine love takes interest in the sorrows and joys of others, and it teaches us to make the feelings of others our own. We are reminded in Hebrews 13:16 of the importance and significance of doing good and sharing:

> But do not forget to do good and to share, for with such sacrifices God is well pleased.

Our prayer for you today is that you experience the comfort of God and share it with others.

> Blessed be the God and Father of our Lord Jesus Christ, the Father of mercies and God of all comfort, who comforts us in all our tribulation, that we may be able to comfort those who are in any trouble, with the comfort with which we ourselves are comforted by God.
>
>   — 2 CORINTHIANS 1:3–4

PERSONAL REFLECTIONS:

- Why do you rejoice with those who rejoice?
- What makes you weep with those who weep?
- How do you do good and share with others?

JANUARY 9

The Power Of Praise And Worship

And do not be drunk with wine, in which is dissipation; but be filled with the Spirit, speaking to one another in psalms and hymns and spiritual songs, singing and making melody in your heart to the Lord, giving thanks always for all things to God the Father in the name of our Lord Jesus Christ, submitting to one another in the fear of God.

— EPHESIANS 5:18–20

"Be filled with the Spirit" is not just a suggestion in the verse above, but it is actually a command—be filled! Paul is reminding us that only by the Holy Spirit are we able to declare the value and worth of God. And when we declare the value and worth of God, we recognize the Person and power of Jesus. We join forces with the Holy Spirit to bring glory and honor to Jesus Christ.

The verses in Ephesians also tell us that we are to sing

songs *out of our spirits* and to make music *in our hearts.* Notice the emphasis is in our hearts. We are spiritual beings. The center of our bodies is the place where our spirits reside. So we sing or praise out of our hearts (the depths of our being).

Notice also that the recommended actions of Ephesians 5:18–21 are vocal: sing, make music, speak to one another, give thanks. The process of being filled with the Spirit requires that we speak, sing, and declare things out of our spirits. The Holy Spirit is released out of our inner beings like a flood or a raging river (John 7:37–38) as we speak out our praises to God.

When we are filled with the Spirit, we will have a desire to worship God and to encourage others in their worship of God.

Our prayer for you today is that you would experience the power of praise and worship, and encourage others to do the same.

PERSONAL REFLECTIONS:

- What does it mean to be filled with the Spirit?
- How do you make music in your heart?
- Do you have a time of praise and worship every day? Why or why not?

JANUARY 10

Utterly Helpless

When we were utterly helpless, Christ came at just the right time and died for us sinners.

— ROMANS 5:6 NLT

Have you ever felt utterly helpless? The apostle Paul is describing helpless ones as those who are unable to save themselves. The utterly helpless sinner is the one for whom Jesus died. Paul spent the first two chapters of the book of Romans telling us that we *all* are utterly helpless sinners.

Paul is also describing the greatness of God's love. It is love given to the undeserving, to those without strength, to the ungodly, to sinners. This should remind us of the fact that the reason for God's love is found *in Him*, not in us.

The demonstration of God's love isn't displayed so much in that Jesus died, but it is seen when we look at the ones for whom He died—the utterly helpless, undeserving sinners and rebels against Him.

> "For the Son of Man has come to seek and to save that which was lost."
>
> — LUKE 19:10

If we don't understand the condition of our hearts without God, we will not be able to comprehend the level of His love and forgiveness.

Our prayer for you today is that you would rejoice in this:

> For he has rescued us from the kingdom of darkness and transferred us into the Kingdom of his dear Son, who purchased our freedom and forgave our sins.
>
> — COLOSSIANS 1:13–14 NLT

PERSONAL REFLECTIONS:

- What does being utterly helpless mean to you?
- Why did Jesus die for sinners?
- How would you describe the greatness of God's love?

JANUARY 11

God Prepares

But as it is written: "Eye has not seen, nor ear heard, nor have entered into the heart of man the things which God has prepared for those who love Him."

— 1 CORINTHIANS 2:9

What does your future look like? We know one thing—life will not be boring for those who know and love the Lord Jesus Christ. What God has prepared for His people is filled with a hope and a future.

For I know the thoughts that I think toward you, says the LORD, thoughts of peace and not of evil, to give you a future and a hope.

— JEREMIAH 29:11

What God has prepared for us is filled with righteousness, peace, and joy.

For the kingdom of God is not eating and drinking, but righteousness and peace and joy in the Holy Spirit.

— ROMANS 14:17

Do you believe that the Creator of all things, the Almighty God, has a plan for you? He does, and all you have to do is respond, "Here I am. Use me." How awesome it is to know He chooses to use people like you and me. He used fishermen. He used farmers and shepherds. He used tax collectors. He gives us all a choice. We can ignore Him and reject His plan, or we can surrender our lives to His purpose and plan. How awesome to think we can be ambassadors for Christ.

Now then, we are ambassadors for Christ, as though God were pleading through us: we implore *you* on Christ's behalf, be reconciled to God. For He made Him who knew no sin *to* be sin for us, that we might become the righteousness of God in Him.

— 2 CORINTHIANS 5:20–21

Our prayer for you today is that you would be encouraged, knowing God has prepared plans for those who love Him. Get ready for the great adventure!

PERSONAL REFLECTIONS:

- What do you think God has prepared for you today?
- What does your future look like?
- Do you have it in your heart to say, "Here am I. Use me"?

JANUARY 12

Being A Good Example

Brethren, join in following my example, and note those who so walk, as you have us for a pattern.

— PHILIPPIANS 3:17

Are you an example? Whether you want people to watch you or not, they are. In other words, being an example is not optional, but what kind of an example you are is.

The more you receive or the greater the position you achieve, the higher the expectations from God and from man. It is an awesome responsibility to be a leader. As a leader, all eyes are upon you, expecting production, perfection, and performance.

Could it be possible for leaders to live in the land of plenty and starve to death for lack of nourishment? When leaders neglect the daily nourishment of their soul with the Word of God, they become spiritually anemic and vulnerable.

However, well-nourished leaders become a rich resource to their disciples (followers).

Our prayer for you today is that you would be found faithful and be able to say,

I press toward the goal for the prize of the upward call of God in Christ Jesus.

— PHILIPPIANS 3:14

PERSONAL REFLECTIONS:

- What does it mean to be an example?
- How do you imitate Christ?
- What does daily nourishment look like to you?

JANUARY 13

He Restores My Soul

He restores my soul; He leads me in the paths of righteousness for His name's sake.

— PSALM 23:3

Does your soul need to be restored? We're all aware of people who are facing painful and devastating circumstances. Gun violence, gang rapes, robberies, and murders. It's all senseless and causing families to be divided and broken. How do we cope under such pressure and hopeless situations? How can we be restored?

In Hebrew, "He restores my soul" can also mean *He restores my life*. The Great Shepherd is the restorer of life for the body as well as the soul. In His mercy, the Shepherd also restores our lives if we go astray. We need our Shepherd's tender and restoring mercy. He so gently brings us into His love and life. Jesus reminded His disciples of this:

I am the door. If anyone enters by Me, he will be saved, and will go in and out and find pasture. The thief does not come except to steal, and to kill, and to destroy. I have come that they may have life, and that they may have it more abundantly.

— JOHN 10:9–10

The Greek word for *abundance* is *perissos*, and it has a mathematical meaning. Generally speaking, *perissos* has the idea of surplus. The abundant life is above just getting by. This provision of life is based upon the fact that God is more than able to meet every emergency and to supply all our needs according to the riches of His glory in Christ Jesus. In other words, His restoring power is abundant in supply.

Our prayer for you today is that you would have hope in His plan and restoring power.

PERSONAL REFLECTIONS:

- What does it mean to be restored?
- How is the Great Shepherd restoring your soul?
- How often do you need His restoring mercy?

JANUARY 14

He Himself Will Rule

He was clothed with a robe dipped in blood, and His name is called The Word of God. And the armies in heaven, clothed in fine linen, white and clean, followed Him on white horses. Now out of His mouth goes a sharp sword, that with it He should strike the nations. And He Himself will rule them with a rod of iron. He Himself treads the winepress of the fierceness and wrath of Almighty God. And He has on His robe and on His thigh a name written: KING OF KINGS AND LORD OF LORDS.

— REVELATION 19:13–16

In your worldview, does Jesus have all authority in heaven and earth? At the return of Jesus Christ, every earthly (former and present) king, president, prime minister, ambassador, congressman, senator, and judge will give account to the KING OF KINGS AND LORD OF LORDS.

Until the return of Christ, we will all have to endure some temporary acts of injustice, manipulation, and divisiveness. However, we must remember that these plans are not eternal.

> For our light affliction, which is but for a moment, is working for us a far more exceeding *and* eternal weight of glory, while we do not look at the things which are seen, but at the things which are not seen. For the things which *are* seen are temporary, but the things which are not seen *are* eternal.
>
> — 2 CORINTHIANS 4:17–18

People who are motivated by envy, hatred, and deceit don't understand the responsibility they have in giving an account to the One who rules with a rod of iron. Verse 15 reminds us a sharp sword goes out of His mouth, and He will "strike the nations." He comes as King of kings to displace every king reigning on this earth. Jesus comes to rule and to reign in triumph, to rule the nations with a rod of iron as predicted in Psalm 2:1–5:

> Why do the nations rage, and the people plot a vain thing? The kings of the earth set themselves, and the rulers take counsel together, against the LORD and against His Anointed, *saying*, "Let us break their bonds in pieces and cast away their cords from us." He who sits in the heavens shall laugh; the Lord shall hold them in derision. Then He shall speak to them in His wrath, and distress them in His deep displeasure.

Our prayer for you today is that you would have a greater understanding of the power and authority of Jesus Christ, and look forward to His return.

PERSONAL REFLECTIONS:

- How would you describe Jesus' reign?
- What "light afflictions" are you having to endure?
- What does it mean that "the Lord shall hold them in derision"?

JANUARY 15

Before Abraham Was, I AM

Then the Jews said to Him, "Now we know that You have a demon! Abraham is dead, and the prophets; and You say, If anyone keeps My word he shall never taste death. Are You greater than our father Abraham, who is dead? And the prophets are dead. Who do You make Yourself out to be?" Jesus answered, "If I honor Myself, My honor is nothing. It is My Father who honors Me, of whom you say that He is your God. Yet you have not known Him, but I know Him. And if I say, I do not know Him, I shall be a liar like you; but I do know Him and keep His word. Your father Abraham rejoiced to see My day, and he saw *it* and was glad." Then the Jews said to Him, "You are not yet fifty years old, and have You seen Abraham?" Jesus said to them, "Most assuredly, I say to you, before Abraham was, I AM." Then they took up stones to throw at Him.

— JOHN 8:52–59

God told Abraham, the father of the Jewish nation, that through him all nations would be blessed (Genesis 12:1-7; 15:1-21). The Jewish leaders, of John's day, did not fully comprehend what the fulfillment of this prophecy was. Abraham had been able to see this through the eyes of faith. Jesus, a descendant of Abraham, became the ultimate fulfillment of this promise.

The statement, "Before Abraham was, I AM," is one of the most powerful statements uttered by Jesus. When He said He existed before Abraham was born, He undeniably proclaimed His divinity. Not only did Jesus say that He existed before Abraham, He also applied God's holy name ("I AM") to Himself. In other words, Jesus claimed to be the great I AM, the Voice of the covenant God of Israel revealed in the burning bush (Exodus 3:13-14).

It is important to understand that, by using the phrase "I AM" (John 8:24, 58; 13:19), Jesus used a clear divine title belonging to Yahweh alone (Exodus 3:13-14; Deuteronomy 32:39; Isaiah 43:10). "I AM" was interpreted as the divine title by Jesus' listeners (John 8:58-59). The Jewish leaders tried to stone Jesus for blasphemy because He claimed equality with God. In accordance with the law in Leviticus 24:16, the religious leaders were ready to stone Jesus for claiming to be God. But Jesus could not deny who He was, is, and is to come.

> "I am the Alpha and the Omega, *the* Beginning and *the* End," says the Lord, "who is and who was and who is to come, the Almighty."
>
> — REVELATION 1:8

Our prayer for you today is that you would continue to proclaim that Jesus is the promised Messiah.

Whoever confesses that Jesus is the Son of God, God abides in him, and he in God.

— 1 JOHN 4:15

PERSONAL REFLECTIONS:

- What do you make of the statement, "Before Abraham was, I AM"?
- Why did the religious leaders want to stone Jesus?
- Who is Jesus?

JANUARY 16

Take Pleasure In

Therefore I take pleasure in infirmities, in reproaches, in needs, in persecutions, in distresses, for Christ's sake. For when I am weak, then I am strong.

— 2 CORINTHIANS 12:10

Do you take pleasure in your affirmities? Not many of us do! However, Paul is giving us a new perspective that can help us see the big picture.

Let's take a moment to give an outline of the biblical usage of the word *pleasure*:

- seems good to one, is one's good pleasure, think it good, choose, determine, decide.
- to do willingly
- to be ready to, to prefer, choose rather
- to be well pleased with, take pleasure in, to be favorably inclined towards one.

What do you take pleasure in? The apostle Paul had a transformation in his life. He no longer looked upon his afflictions as a curse but saw them as a blessing. He goes so far as to boast in them or to praise God for them. He stated in 2 Corinthians 12:9b:

> Most gladly will I boast in my infirmities that the power
> of God may rest upon me.

In other words, he looked beyond the weakness and the pain to the beautiful fruit that God was bringing into his life. Paul's weakness forced him to stay close to God so he might experience God's grace and strength.

How you deal with infirmities, reproaches, needs, persecutions, and distresses will reveal your heart. Only God can transform our thinking so that we can take pleasure in our infirmities. We must have faith to believe God is working out something bigger than what we can see. We take pleasure in knowing this:

> And we know that all things work together for good to
> those who are the called according to *His* purpose.
>
>   — ROMANS 8:28

> And He said to me, "My grace is sufficient for you, for
> My strength is made perfect in weakness." Therefore
> most gladly I will rather boast in my infirmities, that the
> power of Christ may rest upon me.
>
>   — 2 CORINTHIANS 12:9

Our prayer for you today is that you would know the power of His all-sufficient grace.

PERSONAL REFLECTIONS:

- How do you deal with infirmities?
- Is it possible to take pleasure in your infirmities?
- Do you believe God is working out His good in you?

JANUARY 17

Pray Without Ceasing

Rejoice always, pray without ceasing, in everything give thanks; for this is the will of God in Christ Jesus for you.

— 1 THESSALONIANS 5:16–18

Why pray without ceasing? The most important answer is that it is the *will of God in Christ Jesus for us*. When we pray without ceasing, we are recognize the simple truth found in John 15:5,

> "I am the vine, you *are* the branches. He who abides in Me, and I in him, bears much fruit; for without Me you can do nothing."

The word *pray* in "Pray without ceasing" does not mean beg or plead as if God were unwilling to give. Rather, it means by faith to expose every situation as it arises to the One who has *all authority* and who is *all-sufficient*. And most importantly, pray to the One who indwells you. As the apostle Paul reminds us in Galatians 2:20, it's Christ who lives in us.

This being so, applying His grace by faith to every situation as it arises will leave you with no alternative but to obey the other part of 1 Thessalonians 5:18—to give thanks in everything. In how many things? In everything! Without exception, "for this is the will of God in Christ Jesus concerning you."

> **Our prayer for you today is that you would pray without ceasing, knowing who indwells you by His Spirit.**

That good thing which was committed to you, keep by the Holy Spirit who dwells in us.

— 2 TIMOTHY 1:14

PERSONAL REFLECTIONS:

- What can you do to pray throughout the day?
- What can you thank God for today?
- What is the significance of the Spirit in prayer?

JANUARY 18

Walking Worthy Of The Calling

I, therefore, the prisoner of the Lord, beseech you to walk worthy of the calling with which you were called, with all lowliness and gentleness, with longsuffering, bearing with one another in love, endeavoring to keep the unity of the Spirit in the bond of peace.

— EPHESIANS 4:1-3

How do you walk worthy of your calling when there is so much evil around you? Okay, in a non-communist country, we may be entitled to our own opinions. Some call this freedom, some call it liberty, and some call it freedom of speech. However, the truth of the matter is man's opinions seem to come and go like the wind. The reason for this has everything to do with the source of our influence. We need to ask ourselves some questions: "What and who are we being influenced by?" and "What really is the motivation of our hearts in giving our opinions?"

To try to walk worthy (in our calling) without the right source would be, at best, an interesting study in frustration and futility. Unfortunately, it is where our society finds itself today. This is why, as followers of Christ, we must be looking to the Author and Finisher of our Faith. The apostle Paul was dealing with some of the same problems we are facing today. People were being influenced by the wrong sources.

In the world's thinking today, we hear, "I have my truth, and you have your truth." But Jesus said, "I am the truth," and the Bible clearly tells us of a truth that is greater than any individual's feelings about it.

Walking worthy means *walking in humility*.

- Paul speaks of himself as the least of the apostles and not even being worthy of being called an apostle, but he said, "By the grace of God I am what I am."
- In Ephesians 3:8, he referred to himself as less than the least of all the saints.
- In the Greek culture, humility was not considered a virtue. The reason it is considered a virtue by us is that as Christians we live not for our own glory or worldly recognition, but for the glory of our Lord. As Paul said in Galatians 6:14, "God forbid that I should boast except in the cross of our Lord Jesus Christ."

Walking worthy means *walking in meekness or gentleness*.

- Aristotle defined meekness as in between

excessive anger and excessive passivity—
somewhere between being too angry or never
being angry at all.

- There are injustices that should make us angry, but
  we should not be angry over every little thing that
  happens to us.
- The Greek word for *gentleness* is used for an animal
  that has been tamed. The animal's great force is
  brought into submission and obedience to its
  trainer.

Walking worthy means *being long-suffering*.

- The spirit that never gives up, never concedes
  defeat. The Romans did not even think of losing a
  war. They might lose a battle, but they never saw
  themselves as defeated. They believed in ultimate
  victory.
- The second meaning is *patience with men*—the
  spirit that has the power to take revenge but never
  does.

Walking worthy means *bearing with one another in love*. In
the Greek, there are four words for love:

1. *Eros*—passions.
2. *Philia*—emotional love.
3. *Storge*—family love.
4. *Agape*—coined for New Testament, love on the
   spiritual level.

As followers of Christ, our goal should be to walk worthy of our calling rather than rush to share our opinions.

Our prayer for you today is found in the words of the apostle Paul:

I have been crucified with Christ; it is no longer I who live, but Christ lives in me; and the *life* which I now live in the flesh I live by faith in the Son of God, who loved me and gave Himself for me.

— GALATIANS 2:20

PERSONAL REFLECTIONS:

- How are you walking worthy of your calling?
- What does humility look like in your calling?
- Where do you battle being longsuffering?

JANUARY 19

Troubles?

"Let not your heart be troubled; you believe in God, believe also in Me. In My Father's house are many mansions; if it were not so, I would have told you. I go to prepare a place for you. And if I go and prepare a place for you, I will come again and receive you to Myself; that where I am, there you may be also."

— JOHN 14:1–3

Have you ever been surrounded by trouble? Many of us have gone through heartbreaking situations that have caused anxiety, disappointment, and fear. In this passage of Scripture, Jesus had just told His disciples He would be leaving them. He said He would not only go away, but go away in sufferings and reproach. This is one of the main reasons Jesus speaks comfort and vision to His disciples.

Many people in the world are confused and filled with questions today. They may ask things like, "Does anything exist other than the world we live in? Is there life after death? Why do bad things happen to good people?" These troubling questions cannot be understood without recognizing the Creator of the universe and the Giver of life.

The Creator of the heavens and the earth wants us to know His heart. We can take comfort in knowing that, even as He prepares a place for us, Jesus also prepares us for that place. Troubles fade away when we understand God's plan and desire for our lives: "that where I am, there you may be also."

Our prayer for you today is that you would give thanks for this:

The righteous cry out, and the LORD hears, and delivers them out of all their troubles. The LORD *is* near to those who have a broken heart, and saves such as have a contrite spirit. Many *are* the afflictions of the righteous, but the LORD delivers him out of them all.

— PSALM 34:17–19

PERSONAL REFLECTIONS:

- What troubles have you faced and seen God's faithfulness?
- How do you deal with stress?
- What does God's deliverance look like?

JANUARY 20

Who Comforts Us

Blessed be the God and Father of our Lord Jesus Christ,
the Father of mercies and God of all comfort, who
comforts us in all our tribulation, that we may be able to
comfort those who are in any trouble, with the comfort
with which we ourselves are comforted by God.

— 2 CORINTHIANS 1:3–4

It doesn't take people very long to recognize there are
troubles in the world. For those who work in our armed
forces, they are not surprised by the plans going on right
now to produce chaos, destruction, and pain in the nations
of the world. Many of us struggle to watch the devastation
that is a result of actions taken by people who are deceived
and bent on destruction.

For those of us who are parents, it is hard to comprehend,
unless we've been through it, the pain and anguish that
parents go through when facing the loss of a child.

Jesus never told us that we would have life without trouble, but He promised we could have an untroubled heart in a troubled life. He promised to be the God of *all comfort* to us. The word for *comfort* in the New Testament means more than merely soothing someone. It has the idea of strengthening, helping, or making strong. The meaning behind this word is communicated best by the Latin word for *comfort* (*fortis*), which also means *brave*.

The great purpose of God in comforting us is to enable us to bring comfort to others. God's comfort can be given and received through others.

Our prayer is that you would experience comfort from the "Father of mercies and God of all comfort" and share it with others.

PERSONAL REFLECTIONS:

- What comforts you?
- In what way has God comforted you?
- How has God used your trial and testing to comfort others?

JANUARY 21

Approved By God

Remind them of these things, charging them before the Lord not to strive about words to no profit, to the ruin of the hearers. Be diligent to present yourself approved to God, a worker who does not need to be ashamed, rightly dividing the word of truth.

— 2 TIMOTHY 2:14–15

Paul's instruction to Timothy was not for Timothy to present himself approved to *people*, but *to God*. He wasn't to regard the job of being a pastor as a popularity contest but instead as a call to faithfulness *to God*. When Paul mentions to Timothy to present himself "approved to God," he was reminding Timothy that Timothy wasn't to worry so much about presenting other people approved to God (though there was a place for this in his pastoral ministry). His first concern was to present *himself* approved to God.

The focus of Timothy's hard work was this: to rightly divide the Word of God. That is, he had to know what the Word said and didn't say, and how it was to be understood and how it was not to be understood. It wasn't enough for Timothy to know some Bible stories and verses, and then sprinkle them through his sermons as illustrations. His teaching was to "rightly divide" the Word of God and to correctly teach his congregation to do the same. This reminds us of two things:

- Every minister of the gospel must study all the Holy Scriptures from Genesis to Revelation.
- Every minister needs to pray to God, asking Him to show them, through the Holy Spirit, how they must apply His Word to their lives.

Our prayer for you today is that you would be found faithful in rightly dividing God's Word and applying it correctly to your life.

PERSONAL REFLECTIONS:

- How can we be diligent when it comes to the things of God?
- When you think of something approved by God, what do you think of?
- How do you present yourself to God?

JANUARY 22

Made Alive

And you, being dead in your trespasses and the
uncircumcision of your flesh, He has made alive together
with Him, having forgiven you all trespasses, having
wiped out the handwriting of requirements that was
against us, which was contrary to us. And He has taken it
out of the way, having nailed it to the cross. Having
disarmed principalities and powers, He made a public
spectacle of them, triumphing over them in it.

— COLOSSIANS 2:13–15

Wow! Did you just read that? These are some of the most
powerful verses in the Bible! Before a man comes to new
life in Jesus, he is not a sick man who needs a doctor; he is
a dead man who needs a miracle.

Before we have new life in Jesus, we are dead in our trespasses and sins. A trespass is a specific kind of sin: over-
stepping a boundary or missing a mark. We are dead

because we've overstepped God's boundaries in our sin and rebellion.

The great news is Jesus has made us alive "together with Him." In other words, we can't make ourselves alive, but God can make us alive together with Jesus. We can never be made alive apart from Jesus. The "handwriting of requirements" lists our crimes or moral debt before God, a debt that no imperfect person can pay on his or her own. But it can be taken out of the way, by payment from our Lord and Savior, Jesus Christ.

Jesus not only *paid* for the writing that was against us; He also took "it out of the way," and then "nailed it to the cross." He did everything possible to make certain that the "handwriting of requirements that was against us" could no longer condemn us.

Our prayer for you today is that you would know the joy of being "made alive" with Him.

PERSONAL REFLECTIONS:

- What does it mean to be dead in your tresspasses?
- How has He made you alive?
- How has Jesus disarmed principalities and powers?

JANUARY 23

Salt Is Good?

"For everyone will be seasoned with fire, and every sacrifice will be seasoned with salt. Salt is good, but if the salt loses its flavor, how will you season it? Have salt in yourselves, and have peace with one another."

— MARK 9:49–50

Do you like salt? It's pretty hard to eat certain foods without it. Salt has a way of making our food taste just right. However, too much salt or too little salt can mess with our taste buds.

Jesus declared His followers are to be seasoned with fire, and every sacrifice will be seasoned with salt. The salt, however, must retain its flavor to be effective.

We are also reminded in Scripture that our *speech* must be *always with grace seasoned with* this salt, and that no *corrupt communication* may *proceed out of our mouths* (Colossians 4:6). God wants us to communicate His message to the world.

The key is applying the right amount of salt to our communication. In other words, grace makes it savory and keeps it from corrupting.

As followers of Christ, we should be able to answer questions from a biblical perspective, and our communication should be seasoned with grace. The Christian life isn't meant to only be lived in the prayer closet or worship service. It must be practical, lived-out Christianity, which shows communicates grace and truth to those outside the church.

> **Our prayer for you today is that you would "have salt in yourselves, and have peace with one another."**

PERSONAL REFLECTIONS:

- How can you add salt to your communication?
- What does grace seasoned with salt look like?
- Why do we need grace in witnessing to others?

JANUARY 24

The Danger Of Going Alone

And they said, "Come, let us build ourselves a city, and a
tower whose top is in the heavens; let us make a name
for ourselves, lest we be scattered abroad over the face of
the whole earth."

— GENESIS 11:4

The Tower of Babel is the story of self-centered man
against the Creator of heaven and earth. It is man's way of
saying, "We don't need our Creator. We will do things our
own way." This type of thinking is very dangerous. Here
are some observations we can make from the story:

- The reach of human ambition—we all have a
  carnal desire to achieve for ourselves—"Let us
  make a name for ourselves."
- The pride of a self-made reputation—"make a
  name for ourselves" also speaks of ownership, of
  taking the glory and the praise from the lips of

man for ourselves. The pride of a self-made man ("I did it my way") is dangerous. We can build our church structures, denominations, or worldwide ministries from the motivation of pride.

- The surprise of divine intervention—"God came down" shows us that the Lord sees, inspects, and gets involved. God surprised them by interrupting what they thought was impossible to stop.
- The Lord scatters and stops—He actually sent confusion into the work so the people could not continue on. The Lord may fragment a ministry if it hurts His people. God may not let a self-appointed leader continue for years, destroying thousands of lives. God has power to bring a man or ministry down suddenly.

We find great comfort in knowing that we don't have to walk alone. Jesus promises to never leave us or forsake us (Hebrews 13:5).

Our prayer for you today is that you:

Trust in the LORD with all your heart, and lean not on your own understanding; in all your ways acknowledge Him, and He shall direct your paths. Do not be wise in your own eyes; fear the LORD and depart from evil.

— PROVERBS 3:5–7

PERSONAL REFLECTIONS:

- What is the danger of trying to do things on our own without God?
- How do you guard your heart from self-driven motivation?
- What reminds you that you're not alone?

JANUARY 25

What Is Nothing?

"I am the vine, you are the branches. He who abides in Me, and I in him, bears much fruit; for without Me you can do nothing."

— JOHN 15:5

What is nothing? Anything without significance or blessing —for example, fruitless or meaningless living. We can do things every day without God. But this passage teaches us fruitfulness and meaning in life are results of our abiding in Him.

As we saw in yesterday's reading, the Tower of Babel was built without the blessing of the Lord. Genesis 11:4 was a divine warning about building without God's blessing. They wanted to build something reaching into heaven, but they wanted their own names on it. They wanted to build a city, but they had no idea the Lord would come down and inspect what they were building. They thought that, with the momentum and unity they had, nothing would be impossible for them. Genesis 11:8 simply tells us the Lord scattered them and they stopped building. How many ministries and churches do you know that the Lord has scattered and stopped? We need to hear the lessons from this passage of Scripture.

To guard against doing anything out of selfish ambition or corrupt motivations, and to ensure what we do bears fruit that remains, we need to abide in the Lord. As Jesus said,

> If you abide in Me, and My words abide in you, you will ask what you desire, and it shall be done for you. By this My Father is glorified, that you bear much fruit; so you will be My disciples.
>
> — JOHN 15:7–8

Our prayer for you today is that you would be able to see the truth that without Him you can do nothing.

PERSONAL REFLECTIONS:

- Have you ever done something for God without consulting God?
- Why is it important to recognize your dependency?
- How do we keep our motivations pure?

JANUARY 26

Don't Miss His Goodness!

Oh, that men would give thanks to the LORD for His goodness, and for His wonderful works to the children of men! For He satisfies the longing soul, and fills the hungry soul with goodness.

— PSALM 107:8–9

When you're facing a trial, test, or temptation, don't miss the opportunity to *give thanks* for His goodness. It's easy to give thanks when everything is seemingly going your way. The victory comes when we give the Lord thanks and praise during the storm. We can always find a reason for gratitude before God.

Once, Matthew Henry, the famous Bible commentator, was robbed of his wallet. He wrote in his diary, the night he was robbed, all the things he was thankful about:

- First, that he had never been robbed before.

- Second, that though they took his wallet, they did not take his life.
- Third, because even though they took it all, it wasn't very much.
- Finally, because he was the one who was robbed and not the one who did the robbing.

Oh, that men would give thanks! Why? Because He alone can satisfy your longing soul and fill your hungry soul with goodness.

Our prayer for you today is that you wouldn't miss the opportunity to give thanks for His goodness.

PERSONAL REFLECTIONS:

- How do you give thanks to the LORD?
- When do you find it difficult to give thanks?
- How does the LORD satisfy your longing soul?

JANUARY 27

No Sin?

If we say that we have no sin, we deceive ourselves, and the truth is not in us. If we confess our sins, He is faithful and just to forgive us our sins and to cleanse us from all unrighteousness. If we say that we have not sinned, we make Him a liar, and His word is not in us.

— 1 JOHN 1:8–10

Why is *sin* such a bad word to some people? There is a real push to try to eliminate the idea of sin in the world. The world's thinking goes something like this: *If we don't have to deal with any sin problem, we can be free to live any way we choose.* With such thoughts comes the redefining and removal of God's law and morality.

Many have also said, "I just made a mistake. After all, I'm not perfect. I'm only human," but usually they say such things to *excuse* or *defend* themselves. This is different from knowing and admitting we're *sinners saved by grace*.

To say that we have no sin puts us in a dangerous place because God's grace and mercy are extended to *sinners*, not to those who've only made mistakes or claim they're only human. We receive forgiveness when we can say, "I am a sinner. Lord forgive me of my sin." Sin does not have to keep us from a relationship with God. We can find complete cleansing from *all* unrighteousness as we confess our sins.

To *confess* means "to say the same as." When we confess our sin, we are willing to say the same thing about our sin that God says about it. Jesus' story about the religious man and the sinner in Luke 18:10–14 illustrates this. The Pharisee bragged about how righteous he was, while the sinner asked God to be merciful to him, a sinner.

Our prayer for you today is that you would confess your sins to the One who is faithful and just to forgive you of your sins and cleanse you from all unrighteousness.

PERSONAL REFLECTIONS:

- Do you believe not recognizing sin is dangerous?
- In what ways have you minimized sinful behavior in your life?
- What confession do you need to make to the Lord?

JANUARY 28

All Have Sinned

For all have sinned and fall short of the glory of God.

— ROMANS 3:23

God in His righteousness has no option but to find you and me guilty as sinners (dead in trespasses and sins) and alienated from Him. The good news, however, is more than two thousand years ago God in Christ Jesus stepped out of eternity into time, and there extended to you and me His nailed-pierced hands and feet. He was the Lamb of God who would suffer, "the just for the unjust," to bring us back to God (1 Peter 2:24a).

It is very clear in the Scriptures that being in such a sinful state, the only way we can be *justified* is by His sacrifice. Let's be clear, we can't purchase justification with our good works. So we are justified freely by His grace—His unmerited favor, given to us without regard for what we deserve.

Grace is given purely by the sacrifice of Jesus Christ in His death, burial, and resurrection.

Our prayer for you today is that you would rejoice in this wonderful truth:

But God demonstrates His own love toward us, in that while we were still sinners, Christ died for us. Much more then, having now been justified by His blood, we shall be saved from wrath through Him.

— ROMANS 5:8–9

PERSONAL REFLECTIONS:

- Describe the righteousness of God.
- What does *all* have sinned mean?
- How are we justified by His sacrifice?

JANUARY 29

Keep Your Heart

Keep your heart with all diligence, for out of it spring
the issues of life.

— PROVERBS 4:23

There is great reward to those who guard their hearts,
keeping them for wisdom (as in Proverbs 4:21). They enjoy
life flowing from their hearts, like a pleasant and bountiful
reservoir. If the heart is like a reservoir, then change must
begin there. In other words, if the reservoir is polluted, it
does no good to fix the pipes and the valves that are
connected to the reservoir.

The Bible warns us also to avoid a double heart (Psalm
12:2), a hard heart (Proverbs 28:14), a proud heart (Proverbs
21:4),an unbelieving heart (Hebrews 3:12), a cold heart
(Matthew 24:12), and an unclean heart (Psalm 51:10).

You may have heard this saying before, but it's worth
repeating:

You sow a thought. You reap a deed. You sow a deed. You reap a habit. You sow a habit. You reap a character. You sow a character. You reap a destiny.

This saying is filled with wise principles that can be supported by Proverbs 23:7a, "For as he thinks in his heart, so is he."

Our prayer for you today is that you would sow good thoughts from a heart that is filled with His love and truth.

PERSONAL REFLECTIONS:

- How do you keep your heart?
- What are the dangers of not guarding your heart?
- What are the issues of life?

JANUARY 30

I Shall Not Want

The LORD is my shepherd; I shall not want.

— PSALM 23:1

What happens when the LORD is your Shepherd? You don't lack for what you need! You have His provision and protection.

What happens when the LORD is not your Shepherd? You want. You crave. You are never satisfied, nor are you appreciative for what you have.

We live in a time when a significant portion of our society is in open and defiant rebellion against God. Jesus warned of this day in Matthew 24:12:

Because lawlessness will abound, the love of many will grow cold.

To restore our souls, the Lord brings us back to the essentials of our faith. In John 10:14–16, the Great Shepherd reminds us of His love and the need we have to hear His voice:

> I am the good shepherd; and I know My sheep, and am known by My own. As the Father knows Me, even so I know the Father; and I lay down My life for the sheep. And other sheep I have which are not of this fold; them also I must bring, and they will hear My voice; and there will be one flock and one shepherd.

Without the Great Shepherd, we lose touch with God's presence; we lose faith. When we fail to esteem the Great Shepherd as our first love, we will always find sorrow awaiting us. The Great Shepherd keeps our lives from being dry, desolate, and meaningless. Only in Him, shall we not want.

Our prayer for you today is that you would have an assurance of His provision and presence, and declare in thanksgiving, "The LORD is my shepherd. I shall not want."

PERSONAL REFLECTIONS:

- How would you describe the Great Shepherd?
- What happens to those who are filled with want?
- Do you find daily comfort and contentment with the Shepherd?

JANUARY 31

Perfect Peace

You will keep him in perfect peace, whose mind is stayed
on You, because he trusts in You.

— ISAIAH 26:3

God promises we can have perfect peace and be *kept* in a
place of perfect peace. In Hebrew, the term *perfect peace* is
actually *shalom, shalom*. This shows how, in Hebrew, repetition communicates intensity. It isn't just *shalom*; it is *shalom,
shalom—perfect peace*.

We all want to experience perfect peace, but are we willing
to discipline our minds? How do we keep a mind stayed on
Him? The answer is found in trusting in the LORD, which
is based on our yielding to (obeying) the Spirit of God.

For God did not give us a spirit of timidity or cowardice
or fear, but [He has given us a spirit] of power and of
love and of sound judgment and personal discipline

[abilities that result in a calm, well-balanced mind and self-control].

— 2 TIMOTHY 1:7 AMP

The place of perfect peace comes to the one whose mind is stayed on Him. When we keep our minds stayed—settled upon, established upon—the LORD Himself, then we can be kept in this perfect peace. We are to love the LORD our God with all of our minds (Matthew 22:37). We are transformed by the renewing of our minds (1 Corinthians 2:16; Philippians 2:5). We are not to set our minds on earthly things (Philippians 3:19) but to set our minds on things above (Colossians 3:2).

Satan loves to get our minds on anything except the LORD. If our minds are stayed on ourselves, or our problems, or the problematic people in our lives, or on anything else, we can't have this perfect peace.

Our prayer for you today is that you would experience perfect peace as your mind is stayed on the LORD.

PERSONAL REFLECTIONS:

- What does perfect peace look like in your life?
- How do you keep your mind stayed on the LORD?
- How is your mind renewed?

FEBRUARY 1

Diligence

Be diligent to present yourself approved to God, a worker who does not need to be ashamed, rightly dividing the word of truth.

— 2 TIMOTHY 2:15

What does diligence look like? If it keeps us from being ashamed, it must be worth working towards.

Diligence has the idea of being earnest in pursuing a worthy and important goal. It also conveys the idea of studying with an objective in mind. However, the person who settles for average with no aim to move toward excellence is lacking vision. Our vision determines the course we take, and the diligence we have.

As we established earlier, our goal should not be to present ourselves approved to people but to God. We shouldn't regard our call, as a follower of Christ, to be a popularity contest. We should pursue it in response to a call to faith-fulness to God.

The Bible also reminds us that the work of each follower of Christ will be examined at the judgment seat of Christ (2 Corinthians 5:10). Therefore, we have another motiva-tion to work diligently for the Lord so we will not be ashamed when our work is examined.

Our prayer for you today can be found in the following scriptures:

Keep your heart with all diligence, for out of it *spring* the issues of life.

— PROVERBS 4:23

Not lagging in diligence, fervent in spirit, serving the Lord.

— ROMANS 12:11

PERSONAL REFLECTIONS:

- What does diligence look like?
- What does it mean to be ashamed?
- Why is diligence important to you?

FEBRUARY 2

The Correct Appointment

For God did not *appoint* us to wrath, but to *obtain* salvation through our Lord Jesus Christ, who died for us, that whether we wake or sleep, we should live together with Him.

— 1 THESSALONIANS 5:9–10

In the verse above, Paul put two related ideas side-by-side. *Appoint* emphasizes God's sovereignty, and *obtain* is a word that can emphasize human effort. Together, they show the full scope of salvation involves both divine initiative and human responsibility (our will).

Before we had *the hope of salvation*, we had an appointment to wrath. We were appointed to wrath in two ways. First, because of what Adam did to us, we were appointed to wrath (see Romans 5:14–19). Second, because of our own sin, we were appointed to wrath. When Jesus died on the cross, He stood in our place, in our appointment to wrath, and rescheduled us with an appointment to obtain salvation. As believers, when we think we are appointed to wrath, we show up for an appointment that was cancelled by Jesus. The scriptures so beautifully convey that Christ died for us. The idea is that *Jesus died in our place.* Jesus didn't die for us as a favor; He died as our *substitute*.

Hallelujah! We no longer have an appointment to wrath but now an appointment to obtain salvation through our Lord Jesus Christ.

We must remember the responsibility that we each bear. It is the responsibility of "whoever calls on the name of the Lord":

> For "whoever calls on the name of the LORD shall be saved."
>
> — ROMANS 10:13

> "For God so loved the world that He gave His only begotten Son, that whoever believes in Him should not perish but have everlasting life."
>
> — JOHN 3:16

> Whoever believes that Jesus is the Christ is born of God, and everyone who loves Him who begot also loves him who is begot of Him.
>
> — 1 JOHN 5:1

These verses call us to respond to the correct appointment! Don't be late!

Our prayer for you today is that you would know the appointment:

to which He called you by our gospel, for the obtaining of the glory of our Lord Jesus Christ.

— 2 THESSALONIANS 2:14

PERSONAL REFLECTIONS:

- How would you describe God's wrath?
- Why did God not appoint us to wrath?
- How did you obtain salvation through our Lord Jesus Christ?

FEBRUARY 3

The Bible—Corrects Us When We Are Wrong

All Scripture is inspired by God and is useful to teach us
what is true and to make us realize what is wrong in our
lives. It corrects us when we are wrong and teaches us to
do what is right. God uses it to prepare and equip his
people to do every good work.

— 2 TIMOTHY 3:16–17 NLT

How do you respond to correction? We are convinced individuals who don't welcome correction in their lives are
doomed for failure. For a disciple of Christ to make
progress in their growth, they must be open to correction,
having a humble spirit and an appreciative attitude every
day. Receiving correction with appreciation reveals
humility of heart. Rejecting correction reveals a hardened
heart. Proverbs 28:14 says,

Happy *is* the man who is always reverent, but he who
hardens his heart will fall into calamity.

When we come to the Bible and let God speak, teach, correct, and train us, it changes us. It transforms us and our understanding, preparing and equipping us to do every good work. Romans 12:2 says,

> Do not be conformed to this world, but be transformed by the renewing of your mind, that you may prove what *is* that good and acceptable and perfect will of God.

When we let the Bible guide our thinking, our minds are renewed and transformed, so we begin to actually think like God.

We are under the authority of the Word of God. When the Bible exposes something wrong in our lives, we need to respond in humility. The Bible will lead us into everything we need, as long as we respond well to instruction and correction.

Our prayer for you today is that you might be instructed in the right way to live, that your life might be pleasing to God, and that you might live in fellowship with Him.

PERSONAL REFLECTIONS:

- Why do we need correction?
- How do you respond to correction?
- What is the goal of correction?

FEBRUARY 4

The Crown

For I am already being poured out as a drink offering, and the time of my departure is at hand. I have fought the good fight, I have finished the race, I have kept the faith. Finally, there is laid up for me the crown of righteousness, which the Lord, the righteous Judge, will give to me on that Day, and not to me only but also to all who have loved His appearing.

— 2 TIMOTHY 4:6–8

We grew up singing the song "Crown Him with Many Crowns." There are two words used for *crown* in the New Testament. One refers to a royal crown, and the other to the victor's crown (the *stephanos*). Here, Paul referred to the victor's crown—the crown that was essentially a trophy, recognizing that one had competed according to the rules and had won the victory.

Before Paul was a Christian, he supervised the execution of

the first martyr: *Stephanos* (Stephen). He then began to kill as many other Christians as he could. At the end of his life, he was ready to receive a crown—a *stephanos*. It is likely that Paul remembered the name of Stephen.

According to James 1:12, we are promised the *crown of life* if we will endure temptation.

> Blessed *is* the man who endures temptation; for when he has been approved, he will receive the crown of life which the Lord has promised to those who love Him.

This promise is for us—*if* we will set our focus on Jesus, the Author and Finisher of our faith.

Our prayer for you today is that you would experience His grace and strength to endure.

> For you have need of endurance, so that after you have done the will of God, you may receive the promise.
>
>   — HEBREWS 10:36

PERSONAL REFLECTIONS:

- What does a crown symbolize?
- Who will receive the crown of life?
- Why is it important to endure temptation?

FEBRUARY 5

Behave

Love suffers long and is kind; love does not envy; love does not parade itself, is not puffed up; does not *behave* rudely, does not seek its own, is not provoked, thinks no evil; does not rejoice in iniquity, but rejoices in the truth;.

— 1 CORINTHIANS 13:4–6

When we were kids, there was this comic strip in the Sunday newspaper entitled, "Love Is..." It had such a following that there was merchandise to purchase as well as a cartoon in its honor. Why? People were and still are hungry for love.

The apostle Paul was not writing about how love feels, he was writing about how it can be seen in action. True love is always demonstrated by action, not merely by lofty words. When we demonstrate God's love, it will be seen in simple acts of kindness. And by the way, love in action can work anonymously. It does not have to have the limelight or the attention to do a good job, or to be satisfied with the result. Love gives because it loves to give, not out of the sense of praise it can have from showing itself off. Love is always others-focused. Paul communicates the same idea in Romans 12:10 where he says, "in honor giving preference to one another." Also, in Philippians 2:4, it carries the same thought:

> Let each of you look out not only for his own interests, but also for the interests of others.

Being an *others-centered* person instead of a *self-centered* person is truly being like Christ. And when we are Christ-like, we will not behave rudely.

Our prayer for you today is that you will be able to say,

> We give no offense in anything, that our ministry may not be blamed.

> — 2 CORINTHIANS 6:3

PERSONAL REFLECTIONS:

- How would you define love?
- What does behaving rudely look like?
- Why should we be others-centered?

FEBRUARY 6

If You Forgive

"If you forgive those who sin against you, your heavenly Father will forgive you. But if you refuse to forgive others, your Father will not forgive your sins."

— MATTHEW 6:14–15 NLT

Is forgiveness hard for you? You'd be abnormal if you said *no*. Often, we share with others that forgiveness is nothing short of a miracle.

In Matthew 6, the emphasis is on the *imperative* of forgiveness. In other words, forgiveness is not an option. Forgiveness is required for those who have been forgiven. We are not given the luxury of holding on to our bitterness toward other people. It's no wonder that Jesus taught us to pray:

Give us this day our daily bread. And forgive us our debts, as we forgive our debtors.

— MATTHEW 6:11–12

One of the reasons we pray for forgiveness is simply because we need help. Receiving and extending forgiveness is not natural but supernatural. When we have sinned against someone, we either go into denial or experience guilt and condemnation. When we've been hurt and wounded by someone, we find it easy to hold a grudge. We cannot forgive in our own strength. We need help from the LORD.

Jesus has much more to say about forgiveness (see also Matthew 9:2–6; 18:21–35; and Luke 17:3–4). It's a topic we should continue to study and learn more about.

Our prayer for you today is:

"Whenever you stand praying, if you have anything against anyone, forgive him, that your Father in heaven may also forgive you your trespasses."

— MARK 11:25

PERSONAL REFLECTIONS:

- Why is forgiveness difficult at times?
- What should we pray daily?
- Where do you gain strength to forgive?

FEBRUARY 7

Walk In The Spirit

Walk in the Spirit, and you shall not fulfill the lust of the flesh. For the flesh lusts against the Spirit, and the Spirit against the flesh; and these are contrary to one another, so that you do not do the things that you wish. But if you are led by the Spirit, you are not under the law. Now the works of the flesh are evident, which are: adultery, fornication, uncleanness, lewdness, idolatry, sorcery, hatred, contentions, jealousies, outbursts of wrath, selfish ambitions, dissensions, heresies, envy, murders, drunkenness, revelries, and the like ... those who practice such things will not inherit the kingdom of God. But the fruit of the Spirit is love, joy, peace, longsuffering, kindness, goodness, faithfulness, gentleness, self-control.... If we live in the Spirit, let us also walk in the Spirit. Let us not become conceited, provoking one another, envying one another.

— GALATIANS 5:16–26

For those of us who enjoy playing sports, we all have one objective—winning! However, there is one problem: We have an opponent who wants to win as well. Everyone is aware that, to get the win, you have to fight long and hard.

Paul is reminding us that we are in a battle. "For the flesh lusts agains the Spirit, and the Spirit against the flesh." When Paul used the term *flesh*, he didn't mean an actual fleshly body. Instead, Paul used this term to describe the rebellion found in the old nature. Even though the old nature was crucified with Christ, and is dead and gone (Romans 6:6), its influence can still live on in the flesh.

Walking in the Spirit is the key to winning this battle, but it doesn't always come easily. Indeed, it is a fight.

Our prayer for you today is that you would walk in the Spirit so that others would see God's love, joy, peace, longsuffering, kindness, goodness, faithfulness, gentleness, and self-control working through you.

PERSONAL REFLECTIONS:

- How would you describe this battle?
- Which work of the flesh do you find yourself battling today?
- What is your understanding of walking in the Spirit?

FEBRUARY 8

For Whom Do You Live?

And He died for all, that those who live should live no longer for themselves, but for Him who died for them and rose again.... Now then, we are ambassadors for Christ, as though God were pleading through us: we implore you on Christ's behalf, be reconciled to God. For He made Him who knew no sin to be sin for us, that we might become the righteousness of God in Him.

— 2 CORINTHIANS 5:15, 20–21

Since Jesus died for us, it is only fitting that we live for Him. Jesus gave us a new life, not to live for ourselves but to live for Him. The question needs to be asked: Are we living for ourselves, or are we living for Christ?

It is very clear from our opening scripture that God created us for the purpose of living for Him and not for ourselves. It is a corruption of our nature that makes us want to live for ourselves and not for the LORD. Revelation 4:11 says,

> For thou hast created all things, and for thy pleasure they are and were created. We are and were created to live unto God, not unto ourselves. Jesus lived completely unto God the Father.
>
> — KJV

What does living for Christ look like? Living for Christ means living to be His representatives to a lost and dying world. It's a call to be an ambassador, and our mission is to reconcile mankind to God.

Our prayer for you today is that you would know you were created to live for God.

For to me, to live *is* Christ, and to die *is* gain.

— PHILIPPIANS 1:21

PERSONAL REFLECTIONS:

- What does it mean to live for Him?
- When was the last time you did something for someone else, not receiving anything in return?
- How would you describe an ambassador for Christ?

FEBRUARY 9

God Will Reward You

Now, who will want to harm you if you are eager to do good? But even if you suffer for doing what is right, God will reward you for it. So don't worry or be afraid of their threats. Instead, you must worship Christ as Lord of your life. And if someone asks about your hope as a believer, always be ready to explain it. But do this in a gentle and respectful way. Keep your conscience clear. Then if people speak against you, they will be ashamed when they see what a good life you live because you belong to Christ. Remember, it is better to suffer for doing good, if that is what God wants, than to suffer for doing wrong!

— 1 PETER 3:13–17 NLT

For what will God reward you? According to Peter, He will reward you for being *eager to do good.* Just as faith pleases God and brings a award (Hebrews 11:6), so do the actions of doing His good.

Peter reminds us that there is a reward or blessing for us when we suffer for righteousness' sake. God will care for us, especially when we suffer unjustly. Jesus spoke of the same attitude in Matthew 10:28—

> And do not fear those who kill the body but cannot kill the soul. But rather fear Him who is able to destroy both soul and body in hell.

None of us want to suffer. But if we must, may it be for doing good and not for doing evil. The key to suffering will *always* be to keep our eyes on Jesus. Hebrews 12:13 says,

> For consider Him who endured such hostility from sinners against Himself, lest you become weary and discouraged in your souls.

Our prayer for you today is that you would seek to do His good, being bold and gracious as you do it.

> Therefore we also pray always for you that our God would count you worthy of *this* calling, and fulfill all the good pleasure of *His* goodness and the work of faith with power, that the name of our Lord Jesus Christ may be glorified in you, and you in Him, according to the grace of our God and the Lord Jesus Christ.
>
> — 2 THESSALONIANS 1:11–12

PERSONAL REFLECTIONS:

- What does God reward?
- What comes to mind when you think of suffering?
- How does one endure suffering?

FEBRUARY 10

Who Is Your Rewarder?

"For the Son of Man will come in the glory of His Father
with His angels, and then He will reward each according
to his works."

— MATTHEW 16:27

Do you like rewards? We *all* like rewards, raises, and recognition for the work that we have done. However, how many times have you seen someone disappointed for not being recognized for the work they have done? The key to not being disappointed is knowing, loving, and faithfully serving the One who gives the eternal and lasting rewards.

As followers of Christ, we know that, no matter how difficult the work is, we endure because of our desire to receive the reward from the great Rewarder.

Let's read Genesis 15:1, the words God spoke to Abram in a vision:

Do not be afraid, Abram. I *am* your shield, your exceedingly great reward.

God knows how to become the answer to our need. *Whatever* it is, God becomes the provider of that need. When Jesus returns, Revelation 22:12 tells us He will bring His reward with Him, giving to "every one according to his work." If Jesus will give to everyone according to his work, does that mean we are saved by our works? No! But it does show that a living faith will have works with it (James 2:20; Titus 3:8). Here is a simple truth: The work we do becomes a joy in God—the One for whom we are working—rather than what we receive for our work. Christ becomes our reward.

Our prayer for you today is that you would take courage,

knowing that from the Lord you will receive the reward of the inheritance; for you serve the Lord Christ.

— COLOSSIANS 3:24

PERSONAL REFLECTIONS:

- What do you think about rewards?
- Describe the ultimate reward.
- What is Jesus referring to when He say's His reward is with Him?

FEBRUARY 11

Keep Yourself In The Love Of God

But you, beloved, building yourselves up on your most holy faith, praying in the Holy Spirit, keep yourselves in the love of God, looking for the mercy of our Lord Jesus Christ unto eternal life.

— JUDE 1:20-21

Keep yourself in the love of God. With so much envy, jealousy, and hatred all around us, how does we do that? Jude give us three keys on how to keep in the love of God.

- *Build ourselves up on our most holy faith.* This is one way that we can keep ourselves in the love of God. This means that we are responsible for our own spiritual growth. It means that we cannot wait for spiritual growth to just happen, or expect others to make us grow. We need to build ourselves up through reading and studying the Word of God.
- *Pray in the Holy Spirit.* This is another way to keep

ourselves in the love of God. The battle against
wrong living and wrong teaching is a spiritual
battle, requiring prayer in the Holy Spirit.

- *Look for the mercy of Lord Jesus Christ unto eternal life.*
  This is a third way that we can keep ourselves in
  the love of God. As we keep the blessed hope of
  Jesus' soon return alive in our hearts, this
  effectively keeps us in the love of God, and helps
  us to not cast our fath aside.

**Our prayer for you today is that you would keep
yourself in the love of God.**

Now may the Lord direct your hearts into the love of
God and into the patience of Christ.

— 2 THESSALONIANS 3:5

PERSONAL REFLECTIONS:

- How do you build yourself up?
- What does it mean to pray in the Holy Spirit?
- Are you looking forward to the return of Jesus
  Christ?

FEBRUARY 12

Vengeance Is Mine

Beloved, do not avenge yourselves, but rather give place to wrath; for it is written, "Vengeance is Mine, I will repay," says the Lord.

— ROMANS 12:19

If you have experienced a great injustice, it is very difficult not to want to avenge yourself. One of the greatest examples for us in the Old Testament about vengeance and staying guiltless is found in the life of David. At one time, David had the occasion to kill the man (King Saul) who was trying to kill him.

Then Abishai said to David, "God has delivered your enemy into your hand this day. Now therefore, please, let me strike him at once with the spear, right to the earth; and I will not *have* to *strike* him a second time!" But David said to Abishai, "Do not destroy him; for who can stretch out his hand against the LORD's anointed, and be guiltless?" David said furthermore, "*As* the LORD lives, the LORD shall strike him, or his day shall come to die, or he shall go out to battle and perish. The LORD forbid that I should stretch out my hand against the LORD's anointed."

— 1 SAMUEL 26:8–11

It wasn't that David thought Saul was innocent or guiltless. David knew more than anyone that Saul was deeply in sin. But David knew that even a sinning Saul was still the anointed king over Israel (1 Samuel 10:1). He understood it would only change when God changed it; David would not stretch out his hand against the LORD's anointed.

Like David, we can acknowledge that our wrath will not produce the righteousness of God. And like David in Psalm 94:1, we should give the LORD His rightful place:

O LORD God, to whom vengeance belongs—O God, to whom vengeance belongs, shine forth!

Our prayer for you today is found in James 1:19–20,

So then, my beloved brethren, let every man be swift to hear, slow to speak, slow to wrath; for the wrath of man does not produce the righteousness of God.

PERSONAL REFLECTIONS:

- How do you deal with injustice?
- What is usually the result of avenging yourself?
- What does the wrath of God look like?

FEBRUARY 13

By His Grace

But when the kindness and the love of God our Savior toward man appeared, not by works of righteousness which we have done, but according to His mercy He saved us, through the washing of regeneration and renewing of the Holy Spirit, whom He poured out on us abundantly through Jesus Christ our Savior, that having been justified by His grace we should become heirs according to the hope of eternal life.

— TITUS 3:4–7

Are you thankful for His grace in your life? If it weren't for His grace, where would any of us be? We've often said of ourselves that we are imperfect followers of Christ. We love learning about the disciplines in the Christian faith, but we've not always been successful in our application of them. And we think the more we can admit that we have failures and are not always perfect, the more we can experience God's grace.

But He gives more grace. Therefore He says: "God resists the proud, but gives grace to the humble."

— JAMES 4:6

The beauty of God's grace is that it enables us to keep our focus on Christ's power and strength, and not our own weaknesses. This is the essence and distinctive of the gospel. We can notice the emphasis in our opening verses: *of God, not by works, His mercy, He saved us, of the Holy Spirit, He poured, through Jesus, by His grace, heirs.* God is always the initiator, and we receive from Him before we give anything back.

Our prayer for you today is that you would rejoice in knowing:

by grace you have been saved through faith, and that not of yourselves; *it* is the gift of God.

— EPHESIANS 2:8

PERSONAL REFLECTIONS:

- How would you describe the grace of God in your life?
- How has His grace kept you?
- What discipline of grace can you apply to your life today?

FEBRUARY 14

Husbands And Wives

Therefore, just as the church is subject to Christ, so let the wives be to their own husbands in everything. Husbands, love your wives, just as Christ also loved the church and gave Himself for her, that He might sanctify and cleanse her with the washing of water by the word, that He might present her to Himself a glorious church, not having spot or wrinkle or any such thing, but that she should be holy and without blemish. So husbands ought to love their own wives as their own bodies; he who loves his wife loves himself.

— EPHESIANS 5:24–28

"Wow! Think about that kind of love. This is *agape* love. This is unconditional love. This is sacrificial love. This is true love—the same love that Christ showed us by laying down His life for us.

Paul's words to believing husbands safeguards his previous

words to wives. Though wives are to submit to their husbands, it does not give license to husbands to act as tyrants or bullies over their wives. No husband is entitled to say that he is the head of the wife unless he loves his wife to the point of being willing to lay down his own life for her. So the leadership of the husband is to be a leadership of love. It is covering and protection to her.

One of the elders of our church just celebrated their forty-eighth wedding anniversary. Someone asked them the reason for their success, and they shared the following three things that have lended to the longevity of their marriage: *God's love, commitment,* and *respect.* Whether you're married or not, these are three ingredients that grow all relationships.

> **Our prayer for you is that you would experience the grace of God that would enable you to have His love, commitment, and respect in all your relationships.**

PERSONAL REFLECTIONS

1. How does a husband show his love to his wife?
2. What does it mean for a wife to be submitted to her husband?
3. What makes marriage successful?

FEBRUARY 15

Who Does The World Hate?

"The world can't hate you, but it does hate me because I accuse it of doing evil."

— JOHN 7:7 NLT

Who hates Jesus? The world. Why? What evil has He done to it? Jesus boldly confronted the sins of His age and was, therefore, the target of much hatred.

Jesus preached the message of repentance. He told people to "repent, for the kingdom of heaven" was "at hand" (Matthew 4:17). And He said, "For I did not come to call the righteous, but sinners to repentance" (Matthew 9:13).

Despite knowing *all* the world would not receive the Son of God (Jesus Christ) and His Word, we still read these beautiful words:

"For God so loved the world that He gave His only begotten Son, that whoever believes in Him should not

perish but have everlasting life. For God did not send
His Son into the world to condemn the world, but that
the world through Him might be saved."

— JOHN 3:16–17

Those who do not believe are the ones who hate. Those
who hate are those who remain in their rebellion toward
God, denying their sin.

**Our prayer for you today is that you would
embrace the truth:**

If we say that we have no sin, we deceive ourselves, and
the truth is not in us. If we confess our sins, He is
faithful and just to forgive us *our* sins and to cleanse us
from all unrighteousness.

— 1 JOHN 1:8–9

PERSONAL REFLECTIONS:

- Why does the world hate Jesus?
- What does it mean to repent?
- What does it say about a person who is unwilling
  to confess their sin?

FEBRUARY 16

Are You One Of "Those"?

The LORD takes pleasure in *those* who fear Him, in *those* who hope in His mercy.

— PSALM 147:11

In the opening verse, the word *those* is used twice. It's a word we've noticed in a few different verses in the Bible that we're going to look at. But we have a question for you first: Are you one of *those*?

Proverbs 8:17 says,

I love *those* who love me, and *those* who seek me diligently will find me.

Do you love and diligently seek the LORD? Are you one of *those*?

Hebrews 9:27–28 tells us,

And as it is appointed for men to die once, but after this the judgment, so Christ was offered once to bear the sins of many. To *those* who eagerly wait for Him He will appear a second time, apart from sin, for salvation.

Do you eagerly wait for the second coming of the Messiah —Yeshua—the LORD Jesus Christ? Are you one of *those*?

Our prayer for you today is that you would be one of those who fear the LORD, hope in His mercy, love Him, seek Him, and eagerly wait for Him.

PERSONAL REFLECTIONS:

- What does the LORD take pleasure in?
- Who does the LORD love?
- Do you find yourself eagerly waiting for the second coming of Christ?

FEBRUARY 17

What We Find In Prayer

Be anxious for nothing, but in everything by prayer and supplication, with thanksgiving, let your requests be made known to God; and the peace of God, which surpasses all understanding, will guard your hearts and minds through Christ Jesus.

— PHILIPPIANS 4:6–7

How do you guard yourself from being anxious today? The answer is prayer. What we find in prayer is peace.

The Bible describes three great types of peace that relate to God.

- *Peace from God*—Paul continually used this phrase as an introduction to his letters. It reminds us that our peace comes to us as a gift from God.
- *Peace with God*—This describes a relationship that we enter into with God through the finished work

of Jesus Christ. Second John 1:3 describes what comes from that relationship: "Grace, mercy, and peace will be with you from God the Father and from the Lord Jesus Christ, the Son of the Father, in truth and love."

- *The Peace of God*—This is the peace spoken of in our opening verses. It is beyond our power of comprehension. This peace comes from prayer. Don't try to live without it. Don't allow the busyness of life keep you from it. Rather, let His Word be your source of understanding. *Pray* to make it through the day!

Our prayer for you today is that you pray without ceasing so that you stay in the peace of God.

PERSONAL REFLECTIONS:

- Would you describe peace as a gift?
- Where do you find peace?
- What will you do to obtain peace today?

FEBRUARY 18

He Who Believes Will Not Be Put To Shame

That if you confess with your mouth the Lord Jesus and believe in your heart that God has raised Him from the dead, you will be saved. For with the heart one believes unto righteousness, and with the mouth confession is made unto salvation. For the Scripture says, "Whoever believes on Him *will not be put to shame.*"

— ROMANS 10:9–11

Do you battle shame? Many of us battle shame, and the enemy of our souls wants to keep us in this state of disgrace. Shame is defined in the following ways:

- The painful feeling arising from the consciousness of something dishonorable, improper, ridiculous, etc., done by oneself or another: *She was overcome with shame.*
- Disgrace; ignominy: *His actions brought shame upon his parents.*

- A fact or circumstance bringing disgrace or regret: *The bankruptcy of the business was a shame. It was a shame you couldn't come with us.*

We have a real enemy whose work is to bring us into condemnation so that we continue to experience shame. The good news is that Jesus Christ came to destroy the works of the evil one (1 John 3:8). John reminds us that Jesus came to overcome the destruction and condemnation of the devil. Jesus came to put a stop to all this by overcoming the devil completely by His life, suffering, death, and resurrection.

The apostle Paul reminds us:

> *There is* therefore now no condemnation to those who are in Christ Jesus, who do not walk according to the flesh, but according to the Spirit. For the law of the Spirit of like in Christ Jesus has made me free from the law of sin and death.
>
> — ROMANS 8:1–2

And the apostle Peter said,

> Therefore it is also contained in the Scripture, "Behold, I lay in Zion a chief cornerstone, elect, precious, And he who believes on Him will by no means be put to shame."
>
> — 1 PETER 2:6

This is the beauty of believing—there is no more shame!

For the Scripture says, "Whoever believes on Him will not be put to shame."

— ROMANS 10:11

Our prayer for you today is that you would experience a life without shame in Jesus.

PERSONAL REFLECTIONS:

- What does shame look like?
- Who is the one who does not experience condemnation? Why?
- How do you battle shame?

FEBRUARY 19

The Power Of Light

"For everyone practicing evil hates the light and does not come to the light, lest his deeds should be exposed. But he who does the truth comes to the light, that his deeds may be clearly seen, that they have been done in God."

— JOHN 3:20–21

Do you like the light? Unfortunately, some people do not want their lives to be exposed to God's *light* because they are afraid of what will be revealed. Others don't want to be changed because they are enjoying their sin. Don't be surprised when these same people are threatened by your desire to obey God and do what is right. The truth is they are afraid that the light in you will expose some of the darkness in them. They may have to unfollow you on Facebook or avoid you in public, but don't be discouraged. Keep praying that they will come to see how much better it is to live in the light than in the darkness. Don't forget the love and patience of God that was shown you. In other words, remember where you have come from:

> For when we were still without strength, in due time Christ died for the ungodly.
>
> — ROMANS 5:6

> But God demonstrates His own love toward us, in that while we were still sinners, Christ died for us.
>
> — ROMANS 5:8

> For you were once darkness, but *now you* are light in the Lord. Walk as children of light.
>
> — EPHESIANS 5:8

Our prayer for you today is that you would walk in the light.

PERSONAL REFLECTIONS:

- How will you let your light shine today?
- With whom will you share your light?
- In what ways can you show others grace?

FEBRUARY 20

Through The Grace Given

For I say, through the grace given to me, to everyone who is among you, not to think of himself more highly than he ought to think, but to think soberly, as God has dealt to each one a measure of faith.

— ROMANS 12:3

"Amazing grace how sweet the sound"! Is his grace still amazing to you today? We can never forget that grace is a gift from God and that to *each one* has been given *a measure of faith*. When we see ourselves as we really are and realize God has gifted us with grace and faith, it is less likely we will be given over to pride.

Paul does not tell the Christian to take an attitude that finds pleasure in humiliation or degradation. Rather, the idea is that we should see the truth about ourselves and live in light of it. James 4:6 reminds us:

But He gives more grace. Therefore He says: "God resists the proud, but gives grace to the humble."

Love and humility will show itself as we give to one another what God has given to us as gifts. As we do this, we become good stewards of the multi-faceted (manifold) grace of God. Remember, as we serve one another, we do it with the strength God provides and the ability which God supplies so that receives all the glory and honor forever and ever.

Our prayer for you today is that as you have:

received a gift, minister it to one another, as good stewards of the manifold grace of God.

— 1 PETER 4:10

PERSONAL REFLECTIONS:

- What makes grace amazing to you?
- Why is humility so important?
- What does it mean to be "good stewards of the manifold grace of God"?

FEBRUARY 21

The Source Of Love

We love Him because He first loved us.

— 1 JOHN 4:19

We love Him! And we should be unafraid to proclaim it. Can you say, "I love Jesus," to anyone and not be ashamed? Could you imagine a follower of Christ saying, "I love Jesus, but I do not want others to know that I love Him because I'm afraid they will make fun of me."

Why do we love God? The answer is this, because He first loved us. In other words, love was initiated by God. It comes from Him. Our love for God is *always* in response to His love for us. He initiates, and we respond. We never have to draw God to us; instead, He draws us to Himself.

Young ladies and young men, if a guy or girl tells you that they love you, you better make sure they know God. How can anyone say they "love" if they don't know its source.

He who does not love does not know God, for God is love.

                             — 1 JOHN 4:8

At the same time, don't just take what they say as truth, watch their actions and listen to what they say. In most cases, actions speak louder than words.

"He who has My commandments and keeps them, it is he who loves Me. And he who loves Me will be loved by My Father, and I will love him and manifest Myself to him."

                             — JOHN 14:21

Our prayer for you today is that you would be unashamed to say, "I love Him because He first loved me."

PERSONAL REFLECTIONS:

- Why do you love Jesus?
- Have you every been ashamed of being a Christian?
- What does it mean that He first loved you?

FEBRUARY 22

The Lord Opened

When I came to the city of Troas to preach the Good News of Christ, *the Lord opened* a door of opportunity for me.... But thank God! He has made us his captives and continues to lead us along in Christ's triumphal procession. Now he uses us to spread the knowledge of Christ everywhere, like a sweet perfume. Our lives are a Christ-like fragrance rising up to God. But this fragrance is perceived differently by those who are being saved and by those who are perishing. To those who are perishing, we are a dreadful smell of death and doom. But to those who are being saved, we are a life-giving perfume. And who is adequate for such a task as this? You see, we are not like the many hucksters who preach for personal profit. We preach the word of God with sincerity and with Christ's authority, knowing that God is watching us.

— 2 CORINTHIANS 2:12, 14–17 NLT

The LORD's opening an opportunity for Paul should serve as a fresh reminder to us that we need to be interested in ministering where God opens the door. The only way our work for God will be blessed is when it is directed by the Him. Just because the LORD opens the door does not mean everything we do will be accepted by everyone. In other words, the message of the gospel is a message of life to some and a message of condemnation to those who reject it (see John 3:17–21).

Next we read, "We are not like the many hucksters." The word *huckster* (or in NKJV *peddling*) has the idea of *adulterating* or *watering down for gain*, and was specifically applied to a wine seller who watered down the wine for bigger profits. Paul was saying we are not to be like others who water down the gospel for gain. Instead, Paul reminds us that we preach the Word with sincerity. *Sincerity* is the ancient Greek word *eilikrineia*, which means *pure* or *transparent*. It can be described as something which can bear the test of being held up to the light of the sun and looked at with the sun shining through it. In other words, the message and ministry should not have hidden agendas.

Like the apostle Paul, we should always be aware that our first audience in ministry is God Himself. Every word we speak, we should remember we speak "knowing that God is watching us."

Our prayer for you today is that you would look to the Lord for open doors, and that He would find you faithful and sincere.

PERSONAL REFLECTIONS:

- What does a door of opportunity mean to you?
- How would you describe a huckster?
- What comes to mind when you read, "God is watching you"?

FEBRUARY 23

The Lamb Of God

The next day John saw Jesus coming toward him, and said, "Behold! The Lamb of God who takes away the sin of the world!"

—JOHN 1:29

In this one verse, John the Baptist summarized the greatest work of Jesus: to deal with the sin problem afflicting the whole world. He is the Lamb of God! Every word of this verse is important.

The Gospel writer, John, used the image of the sacrificial lamb, which was represented many times in the Old Testament. Jesus is the perfect fulfillment every time that the image is displayed. For example:

- He represents the lamb slain before the foundation of the world.

- He represents the lamb that God would Himself provide for Abraham as a substitute for Isaac.
- He represents the Passover lamb for Israel.
- He represents the lamb for the guilt offering in the Levitical sacrifices.
- He represents Isaiah's lamb to the slaughter, ready to be sheared.

Each of these lambs fulfilled their role in their death. John's announcement was that Jesus would die as a sacrifice for the *sin of the world*. The sacrifice of this *Lamb of God* has all the capacity to forgive every sin and cleanse every sinner. The good news is: His sacrifice is big enough for the *whole world*.

> **Our prayer for you today is that you would recognize Jesus as the Lamb of God who takes away the sin of the world.**

PERSONAL REFLECTIONS:

- What are some characteristics of a lamb?
- Describe our need for the Lamb of God.
- What did the Lamb of God provide?

FEBRUARY 24

Peace In The Testing

You will keep him in perfect peace, whose mind is stayed
on You, because he trusts in You.

— ISAIAH 26:3

Do you need perfect peace today? We were praying for our
daughter today as she was preparing for her high school
state testing. We asked God to give her not just peace but
His perfect peace.

In Hebrew, the term *perfect peace* is actually *shalom shalom*.
This shows how, in Hebrew, repetition communicates
intensity. It isn't just *shalom*; it's *shalom shalom*, perfect
peace. God promises that we can have perfect peace, and
even be *kept* in a place of perfect peace.

It's not just our daughter who will face testing today. Most
of us will face various tests throughout the day. The key to
how well we will do is based on our focus. "Whose mind is
stayed on You," this is the place of perfect peace, and the

source of it. When we keep our minds stayed (settled upon, established upon) on the LORD Himself, then we can be kept in this perfect peace. This isn't so much a matter of our spirits, souls, or hearts as it is a matter of our minds. We are to love the LORD our God with all our minds (Matthew 22:37). We are transformed by the renewing of our minds (Romans 12:2). We can have the mind of Christ (1 Corinthians 2:16, Philippians 2:5). We are not to set our minds on earthly things (Philippians 3:19), but to set our minds on things above (Colossians 3:2). Where we set our minds is essential in our walks before the LORD if we are to experience *perfect peace*.

Our prayer for you today is that the God of peace will be with you and that you would experience the peace of God.

PERSONAL REFLECTIONS:

- How would you describe perfect peace?
- Where do you find peace?
- What does having a mind stayed on Him look like?

FEBRUARY 25

Ask, Seek, Knock

"Ask, and it will be given to you; seek, and you will find; knock, and it will be opened to you. For everyone who asks receives, and he who seeks finds, and to him who knocks it will be opened. Or what man is there among you who, if his son asks for bread, will give him a stone? Or if he asks for a fish, will he give him a serpent? If you then, being evil, know how to give good gifts to your children, how much more will your Father who is in heaven give good things to those who ask Him!"

— MATTHEW 7:7–11

What are you asking God for? Some people seek God earnestly only when they are in trouble, but the beauty of spending time in the Word of God daily is that we seek Him intensely all the time.

Ask—seek—knock. We see a progressive intensity going

from ask to seek to knock. Jesus told us to have intensity, passion, and persistence in our relationship with Him.

I've heard it said, "*Ask* with confidence and humility. *Seek* with care and application. *Knock* with earnestness and perseverance." The idea of knocking also implies that we sense resistance. After all, if the door were already open, there would be no need to knock. Yet Jesus encourages us that, even if we sense the door is closed and we must knock, then we do so and continue to do so daily, and we will see the answer.

We've come to believe that God values persistence and passion in prayer because they show that we share His heart. They show that we care about the things He cares about.

Be encouraged, God promises an answer to the one who will diligently ask, seek, and knock.

Our prayer for you today is you would continue to ask the Lord for daily bread.

PERSONAL REFLECTIONS:

- What does it mean to you to ask, seek, and knock?
- What do you desire for God to do in your life?
- How often will you ask, seek, and knock?

FEBRUARY 26

Well Pleasing

Now may the God of peace who brought up our Lord Jesus from the dead, that great Shepherd of the sheep, through the blood of the everlasting covenant, make you complete in every good work to do His will, working in you what is well pleasing in His sight, through Jesus Christ, to whom be glory forever and ever. Amen.

— HEBREWS 13:20–21

The writer of Hebrews starts out with, "Now may the God of peace...." This is known as a *prayer of blessing* similar to the priestly blessing in Numbers 6:24–27:

The Lord bless you and keep you; the Lord make His face shine upon you, and be gracious to you; the Lord lift up His countenance upon you, and give you peace.

In this blessing, God is first recognized in His attributes:

- Peace
- Power (brought up our Lord Jesus from the dead)
- Loving care (that great Shepherd)
- Forever love (the blood of the everlasting covenant).

Next, we read these beautiful words: "Make you complete in every good work." This expresses the outcome of God's blessing. The blessings of God cause us to be fruitful so that the Father is glorified.

> "By this My Father is glorified, that you bear much fruit; so you will be My disciples."
>
> — JOHN 15:8

In other words, God's blessings are the very things He is working in us. What makes us well pleasing to Him is that we embrace His blessings in our lives.

Our prayer for you today is that you would be "well pleasing in His sight, through Jesus Christ."

PERSONAL REFLECTIONS:

- How would you describe the God of Peace?
- What is well pleasing to God?
- Why is it important to be "complete in every good work"?

FEBRUARY 27

Love In Deed And In Truth

But whoever has this world's goods, and sees his brother in need, and shuts up his heart from him, how does the love of God abide in him? My little children, let us not love in word or in tongue, but in deed and in truth.

— 1 JOHN 3:17-18

How do we show love? These verses are direct and to the point. If you have the capability to meet a brother's need and do nothing to meet that need, then how can you say you love that brother? How does the love of God abide in you? John will not allow us to merely talk about love; real love is demonstrated in action.

The other day, we had someone in Cleveland ask us for some money. He said he lost his wallet and needed some help. The questions came to our minds: *Is he telling the truth? What will he use the money for?* And then the ultimate question, *how do we show him God's love?*

We came to the conclusion that day, if we have the capability to meet a brother's need and do nothing to meet the need, then how can we say we love our brother?

Is there a limit to this kind of love? The only limit is the one that love itself imposes. When giving to a person, we need to ask this question: Does the money bring him harm instead of good? If it does, then the loving thing to do is to *not* give him what he asks for, but to give him what he really needs instead. We must all understand God has called us to show love in deed and in truth.

Our prayer for you today is that you would

let love *be* without hypocrisy. Abhor what is evil. Cling to what is good. *Be* kindly affectionate to one another with brotherly love, in honor giving preference to one another; not lagging in diligence, fervent in spirit, serving the Lord; rejoicing in hope, patient in tribulation, continuing steadfastly in prayer; distributing to the needs of the saints, given to hospitality.

— ROMANS 12:9–13

PERSONAL REFLECTIONS:

- How do you show love to others?
- How do you abide in God's love?
- What will you do to meet someone's need today?

FEBRUARY 28

By This We Know Love

By this we know love, because He laid down His life for us. And we also ought to lay down our lives for the brethren.

— I JOHN 3:16

To understand the biblical idea of love, we should begin by understanding the vocabulary of love among the ancient Greeks. They gave us the original language of the New Testament.

- *Eros* was one word for love. It described, as we might guess from the word itself, *erotic* love. It referred to sexual love.
- *Storge* was the second word for love. It referred to family love, the kind of love there is between a parent and child, or between family members in general.
- *Philia* is the third word for love. It spoke of a

brotherly friendship and affection. It is the love of deep friendship and partnership. *Philia* love might be described as the highest love that one is capable of without God's help.

- *Agape* is the fourth word for love. It described a love that loves without changing. It is a self-giving love that gives without demanding or expecting re-payment. It is love so great that it can be given to the unlovable or unappealing. It is love that loves even when it is rejected.

We would not *know* what love was all about if not for the work of Jesus on the cross. No wonder there is such a push to deny that Jesus died and rose from the dead! It isn't the death of Jesus in *itself* that is the ultimate demonstration of love; it is the death of Jesus together with *what it does for us* that shows us the real picture of love. The exact same idea was expressed by Paul in Romans 5:8:

> But God demonstrates His own love toward us, in that while we were still sinners, Christ died for us.

John also reminds us that love and its demonstration often involve *sacrifice*. We may consider ourselves ready to lay down our lives in one great, dramatic, heroic gesture; but for most of us, God calls us to lay down our lives piece by piece, little by little, in small but important ways daily.

Our prayer for you today is found in Philippians 2:3–4:

Let nothing *be done* through selfish ambition or conceit, but in lowliness of mind let each esteem other better than himself. Let each of you look out not only for his own interests, but also for the interests of others.

PERSONAL REFLECTIONS:

- What does love look like?
- How would you define love?
- What is the ultimate demonstration of love?

Made in the USA
Monee, IL
04 November 2020

46703264R00144